Tour the Twilight Saga

Book One:

The Olympic Peninsula

A Novel Holiday Travel Guidebook

By CD Miller

Tour the Twilight Saga Book One:
The Olympic Peninsula
A Novel Holiday Travel Guidebook

By CD Miller

Published by:
A Novel Holiday Travel Guidebooks
16614 226th Street
Ashland, NE 68003
http://www.anovelholiday.com

All rights reserved. No part of this book may be reproduced or transmitted in any form or by any means, electronic or mechanical—including photocopying, recording, or any information storage and retrieval system—without written permission from the author, except for the inclusion of brief quotations in a review.

The publisher and author of *Tour the Twilight Saga* Book One have taken great care to ensure that all information provided is correct and accurate at the time of submission. Unfortunately, errors and omissions—whether typographical, clerical or otherwise—sometimes occur. If you find an error or omission, please Email us and report it.
chas@novelholiday.com

Changes in real-world site information will inevitably occur. As aptly stated by renowned travel guidebook author **Rick Steves**: "Guidebooks begin to yellow even before they're printed." For instance, the ticket and entry fees cited are those that were in effect during our last pass at researching each Twilight Saga Site.

Users of any *Tour the Twilight Saga* travel guidebook are advised to access the Internet links provided within each chapter in order to obtain the most up-to-date information during the planning of your Twilight Saga holiday.

Currency equivalents are offered only to provide an *approximate idea* of what US Dollars ($) equal in British Pounds (£). Currency exchange rates change daily. Check current foreign exchange rates by using a free Internet currency converter such as the one offered by **Oanda**:
http://www.oanda.com/currency/converter/

The publisher and author(s) of *Tour the Twilight Saga* travel guidebooks hereby disclaim any liability to any party for loss, injury, or damage incurred as a direct or indirect consequence of errors, omissions, or post-manuscript-submission information changes, whether such errors, omissions, or changes result from negligence, accident, or any other cause.

Copyright © 2014 by Charly D Miller,
A Novel Holiday Travel Guidebooks Publishing Company
Printed in the United States of America
ISBN 978-1-938285-22-6

Publisher's Cataloging-in-Publication Data
Miller, Charly D, 1956 -
Tour the Twilight Saga Book One: The Olympic Peninsula
by Charly D Miller.
p. cm.

1. Travel Guides—United States—.
I. Title.
F852.3 M460 2014

Disclaimers

Novels as incredibly popular as Stephenie Meyer's *Twilight Saga* series inevitably generate an amazing number of **unauthorized** guides, companion books, philosophical essay collections, and the like. To avoid the threat of copyright or trademark infringement litigation, unauthorized *Twilight Saga*-related books publish at least one **Disclaimer**. Below are the **several** important *Tour the Twilight Saga* Disclaimers.

This is an Unauthorized Twilight Saga Travel Guidebook

Tour the Twilight Saga Book One [hereinafter referred to as **TTTS One**] is not authorized, approved, endorsed, nor licensed by Stephenie Meyer; Summit Entertainment, LLC; Little, Brown and Company; Hachette Book Group, Inc.; Time Warner Book Group; nor by any other persons, entities, corporations or companies claiming a proprietary interest in the *Twilight Saga* books, movies, or related merchandise.

TTTS One is not officially associated with the four *Twilight Saga* novels written and copyrighted by Stephenie Meyer. Nor is TTTS One in any way officially associated with the five *Twilight Saga* movies produced and trademarked by Summit Entertainment.

The Purpose of Tour the Twilight Saga Book One

TTTS One was written solely for the purpose of providing an historical review of, and directions for finding, the real-world Washington State (U.S.), Olympic Peninsula locations mentioned in Stephenie Meyer's novels.

Twilight-Associated Names, Places, Titles or Terminology

TTTS One does not claim, nor does it intend to imply, ownership of, or proprietary rights to, any of the character or place names, titles or terminology, used or created by Stephenie Meyer within her *Twilight Saga* novels, or the movies made thereof.

Publication of *Twilight Saga* Movie Screenshots

Screenshots (aka screen-caps) are split-second, still photographs captured when playing a movie on a computer. Several of the twenty-three (23) Twilight Saga Site chapters in TTTS One include one or more movie screenshots or screenshot segments. The sole purpose of including them is

Tour the Twilight Saga Book One

to enhance the experience of *Twilight Saga* fans [**Twilighters**] while visiting Twilight Saga Sites. By observing screenshots while visiting, Twilighters are reminded of the location as it was seen on screen—even though the movies were filmed elsewhere.

To be an effective reminder of the movie locales, however, the movie screenshots had to be altered in a variety of ways so that the film site's **background** could more easily be recognized.

All five *Twilight Saga* films were produced and trademarked by Summit Entertainment. TTTS One does not claim, nor does it intend to imply, ownership of, or proprietary rights to, any portions of the *Twilight Saga* movies.

The caption of every screenshot and screenshot segment that appears within TTTS One should officially include the following copyright caveat: "™©Summit Entertainment, LLC." Inclusion of that information, however, would cause each screenshot's caption to be two lines long. Because this info is given here, we can save room by captioning screenshots only with identification of the movie from which each was captured.

Using Google Maps to Create *Tour the Twilight Saga* Site Maps

In order to assist visiting Twilighters to find multiple locations within a single TTTS Site chapter—such as the city of Port Angeles, or the Quileute Reservation—we used segments of Google Maps images, then enhanced and augmented them to create a few **TTTS Site Maps** for Book One.

TTTS One authors strictly adhered to the *Google Maps and Google Earth Content Rules & Guidelines*, and appropriately attributed Google with credit for the thumbnail-sized TTTS Site Map images published within the travel guidebook. Said credit also applies to the full-sized TTTS Site Map images included within the Supplement PDFs posted on TourTheTwilightSaga.com.

TTTS One does not claim, nor does it intend to imply, ownership of, or proprietary rights to, any of the Google Maps image segments—or Google Street view image segments—used within the travel guidebook or the Supplement PDFs posted on TourTheTwilightSaga.com.

Author vs Authors of *Tour the Twilight Saga*

The **A Novel Holiday** travel guidebook publishing company concept was solely conceived by Ms. Charly D. Miller, as was the concept of the A Novel Holiday (**ANH**) *Tour the Twilight Saga* travel guidebook series. During the researching and writing of TTTS travel guidebooks—as well as during TTTS website design—Ms. Miller was so generously assisted by other individuals, that she feels unworthy of claiming sole credit for authoring the texts' or websites' content. Thus, **plural terms**—such as, "authors" … "we"

Disclaimers

... "our"—are used throughout TTTS travel guidebooks, and the website, when referring to the writers or creators of same.

For all legal purposes, however, every A Novel Holiday *Tour the Twilight Saga* travel guidebook was solely written by CD Miller. She, alone, is responsible for all content published within any TTTS travel guidebook eBook or paperback, as well as all content posted on the ANH and TTTS websites.

Ms. Charly D Miller hereby avows and affirms that any and all other individuals who participated in or contributed to the researching, writing, or publication of *Tour the Twilight Saga* travel guidebooks and associated websites, are **indemnified and held harmless** from and against: any and all demands, claims, and damages to persons or property, losses and liabilities, including attorney's fees arising out of or caused by any form of litigation brought against the A Novel Holiday *Tour the Twilight Saga* travel guidebooks or websites.

Tour the Twilight Saga Book One

Credits and Acknowledgments

Tour the Twilight Saga Art

Our gorgeous Twilight Saga Logo—and the three Twilight Saga Site Rating Icons—were designed by two terrifically talented graphic artists: **Karen Dale (neé Stoehr)** and **Ben Dale**.

http://www.coroflot.com/dalek/profile
http://bendale.daportfolio.com/

Tour the Twilight Saga Book Cover

DC Carson used a fabulous photo snapped by **Tara Miller** to design the Twilicious TTTS Book One cover.

Photo Credits

Beneath each photograph is a caption containing the name of the person who snapped the pic and the year in which it was taken. Some photos were obtained online from **Wikipedia** or **Wikimedia**, where they were posted by photographers who generously offered the freedom of their commercial re-use. A few photos, however, were obtained from Internet sites that neglected to provide photographer contact information. If we've used *your*

Tour the Twilight Saga Book One

photo without asking permission to do so, please Email us so we can request permission to continue using it.
chas@novelholiday.com

Personal Acknowledgements from Author, CD Miller

Thank you, Tara!

The most dedicated *Tour the Twilight Saga* travel guidebooks contributor is **Ms. Tara Miller** of Findlay, Ohio—*not* a blood relation, but still a *sister*! During the hundreds of Internet research hours she voluntarily performed, Tara helped to discover important Twilight Saga Sites that might otherwise have been missed. Tara also joined me on my September 2013 recon trip of Washington's Olympic Peninsula. Because she takes *far better pix* than I do, Tara's photography was a huge boon to Book One.

Thank You, to All the Others Who Helped

The people listed below generously contributed info and/or pix to *Tour the Twilight Saga* Book One. Their assistance was extremely important to ensuring the accuracy of Book One's content.

- Marcia Bingham and Lissy Andros of the Forks Chamber of Commerce
- Nino, Rosemary, and Jennifer Colandrea of Fork's TwiFoot Tours
- Michelle and John Simpson of Westlands Homestead
- Carol and Matt Hutchison of Searcy, Arkansas—Twilighters we met in Forks!
- Ron Spomer of **www.ronspomeroutdoors.com**

My Biggest Thank You Goes to Ms. Dina C. Carson

As I embark upon the second A Novel Holiday travel guidebook series, I remain more grateful to DC Carson than mere words can possibly convey.

Dina has helped with *all* my ANH travel guidebook projects from the very beginning—back in 2007. She nursed me through the writing of five *Harry Potter Places* travel guidebooks. And now she's helping me with the four *Tour the Twilight Saga* travel guidebooks. Without Dina's incredibly astute writing guidance and editing talents, every ANH travel guidebook would be *awful*.

My fondest wish is to someday be able to reciprocate the favors Dina's performed for me. Unfortunately, because Dina is far more talented than I am at *everything*, it is entirely unlikely that I'll ever be able to help her as she's helped me. Hopefully, however, I'll *SOMEDAY* be able to financially reward her!

Thank you, Thank you, Thank you, Dahlink Dina!

Acknowledgments

To My Personal Friends

Susan and Bob, Jamie, Janet and Mike, Chet, Leeenda and Mike, the Greene Sibdiblings ... these are just a few of the *scores* of people I have to thank! Each of these individuals have contributed—in their own way—to ensuring that I can continue pursuing my ANH travel guidebook projects. You guys have no idea how much I appreciate your help, and how much I value your friendship.

Lastly, to Drew and Annabeth, Auntie Dot and Uncle Itchy

Bless You for always believing in me!

Tour the Twilight Saga Book One

Table of Contents

Title Page and Copyright Information   ii
Disclaimers   iii
Credits and Acknowledgements   vii
Table of Contents   xi

Chapter 1—Introduction
About *Tour the Twilight Saga* Book One   1
The Twilighter Treaty
Twilight Saga Site Rating Icons
TwiLinks
Tour the Twilight Saga Supplements
Twi Travel Tips

Chapter 2—Tips for Twilighting in the Olympic Peninsula
Everything a Twilighter or Twihard needs to know for planning   5
the most Twilicious Olympic Peninsula Twilight Saga Tour possible.

Olympic Peninsula Twilight Saga Sites
Chapter 3—**Seattle:** Site #1   9
Chapter 4—**Port Angeles:** Site #2   41
Chapter 5—**Forks & La Push Prologue**   55
Chapter 6—**Forks Welcome Sign:** Site #3   71
Chapter 7—**Forks Chamber of Commerce:** Site #4   75
Chapter 8—**Forks Outfitters & The Thriftway:** Site #5   85
Chapter 9—**Forks Coffee Shop:** Site #6   89
Chapter 10—**Forks High School:** Site #7   93
Chapter 11—**Leppell's Flowers & Gifts:** Site #8   99
Chapter 12—**Forks Police Department:** Site #9   105

Tour the Twilight Saga Book One

Chapter 13 — The Miller Tree Inn: Site #10   109
Chapter 14 — Native To Twilight: Site #11   115
Chapter 15 — Twifoot Tours: Site #12   119
Chapter 16 — JT's Sweet Stuffs: Site #13   127
Chapter 17 — Sully's Drive-In: Site #14   131
Chapter 18 — Forks Community Hospital: Site #15   133
Chapter 19 — The Swan House: Site #16   137
Chapter 20 — Discarded Motorcycles location: Site #17   141
Chapter 21 — Old Mill Trading Post & the Round House: Site #18   143
Chapter 22 — Treaty Line Sign: Site #19   149
Chapter 23 — Jacob Black's house & The Wolf Den: Site #20   155
Chapter 24 — La Push, First Beach: Site #21   161
Chapter 25 — The Quileute Res & La Push Village: Site #22   181
Chapter 26 — Westlands Homestead: Site #23   203
Index   217

Introduction

Tour the Twilight Saga Book One is designed to guide **Twilighters** (regular Twilight Saga fans) and **Twihards** (*die-hard* Twilight Saga devotees) to Twilight Saga sites located in Washington State's Olympic Peninsula.

No Filming Took Place in the Olympic Peninsula

When researching and writing her first novel, Stephenie Meyer selected the Olympic Peninsula town of Forks, Washington, as the primary setting for *Twilight*. Naturally, locations near to Forks soon crept into her manuscript: La Push First Beach, Port Angeles, the Quileute Reservation, and Seattle.

When plans began for filming, *Twilight* director Catherine Hardwicke hoped to shoot in Forks and the other real-world Olympic Peninsula novel locations. Unfortunately, the first Twilight Saga movie was a relatively low-budget project. Forks' remote location, and Washington State's exorbitant filming fees at the time, ultimately made it far too expensive for her to film at any of the real-world sites.

Thus, all *Tour the Twilight Saga* (**TTTS**) Book One locations are **novel-related places—*not* film sites**.

It is not our intention to diminish the importance of visiting Olympic Peninsula Twilight Saga sites. In fact, we believe that the real-world novel locations are far more exciting and enjoyable than the film sites. We simply want to ensure that Twilighters and Twihards understand that Olympic Peninsula Twilight Saga sites are places described in Stephenie's novels, *not* places you'll recognize from footage seen on screen.

Happily, we'll take you to **Twilight Saga Film Sites** in subsequent TTTS travel guidebooks.
- **Book Two: Vancouver, British Columbia**
- **Book Three: Oregon and Washington**
- **Book Four: USA—and Around the World**
  These locations are found in the US states of California and Louisiana, the countries of Brazil and Italy, as well as **St. Thomas in the US Virgin Islands.**

Tour the Twilight Saga Book One

[Google Maps segments married & enhanced, ©2013 Google]

What is the Olympic Peninsula?

The Olympic Peninsula is the northwestern-most part of the contiguous continental United States. A section of the state of Washington, the Olympic Peninsula is bounded by the Pacific Ocean on the west, the Strait of Jaun de Fuca (a section of the US-Canadian border) in the north, and on the east by the Hood Canal, which lies just west of Puget Sound. The Olympic Peninsula's southern border begins in the approximate area of Aberdeen, Washington—the "Gateway to the Olympic Peninsula."
http://en.wikipedia.org/wiki/Olympic_Peninsula
http://www.olympicpeninsula.org/

Technically, the city of Seattle, Washington (TTTS Site #1) lies outside the Olympic Peninsula's eastern border. For TTTS Book One purposes, however, Seattle is considered part of the Olympic Peninsula.

The Twilighter Treaty

It is important that all Twilighters and Twihards be as polite as possible when visiting Twilight Saga sites, especially those situated on private property.

Introduction

It only takes *one* noisy or disrespectful fan to ruin the reception received by all Twilighters who visit thereafter. Please be the very best **Twilight Saga Ambassador** you can possibly be, and abide by the Twilighter Treaty everywhere you go.

The Twilighter Treaty:
Do not trespass on private property.
Do not disturb—or photograph—the residents.
Do not bite any humans, for any reason.

Twilight Saga Site Rating Icons

One of the reasons *Tour the Twilight Saga* is split into four travel guidebooks is that, as of March 2014, we've discovered *eighty-seven* (87) Twilight Saga Sites in the world. Obviously, not all of them are places even Twihards will want to visit. During our research, we critically assess each site and assign it a site rating based on its degree of Twiliciousness.

  The **Great Site** icon indicates a Twilight Saga Site you don't want to miss.

  The **Might Be Fun** icon identifies places that Twilighters might find interesting, but may not be worth visiting. Each Might-Be-Fun Site has an explanation of why it received that rating.

  The **Skip It** icon is assigned to places we suggest you *don't bother visiting*, and the site's entry explains why. Although addresses or SatNav/GPS coordinates are provided for Skip-It-rated sites, we don't offer directions for finding them, nor are Skip It sites included in any of

Tour the Twilight Saga Book One

our suggested itineraries. Twihards divinely inspired to visit a Skip It site should investigate the location using the information provided in its TTTS Site entry to create their own itinerary.

Happily, of the twenty-three (23) Twilight Saga Sites found in Washington's Olympic Peninsula, *none* are Skip-It-rated, and only *two* are Might-Be-Fun-rated! In other words, TTTS Book One will take you to **all** the **Olympic Peninsula Twilight Saga Sites**.

☙❧

TwiLinks, Supplements, and Twi Travel Tips

TwiLinks are PDFs posted online containing all of the **Internet resource links** provided within each section or chapter of every *Tour the Twilight Saga* travel guidebook. TwiLink PDFs allow you to access websites important to planning a Twilight Saga trip without having to type each Internet resource link's address into your Internet browser. TwiLink files were created to assist Twilighters who purchase a TTTS **paperback**. Twilighters who buy a TTTS **eBook**, but use an eReader from which Internet access isn't convenient, will also find them helpful.

    Supplement PDFs contain site-specific background information and maps.

    Go to **TourTheTwilightSaga.com** and click on the link for **Book One** in the left navigation bar. Then click on Book One's **TwiTips & Maps** link. There you'll find a directory of Book One TwiLinks and Supplements.

Twi Travel Tips contain information important to *all* Twilighters planning to tour Twilight Saga Sites *anywhere* in the world. That directory link is in the left navigation bar at the bottom of each webpage.

Tips for Twilighting in the US Olympic Peninsula

The travel interests and needs of Twilighters or Twihards embarking on a Twilight Saga Tour are terrifically diverse. To keep *Tour the Twilight Saga* travel guidebooks as slim as possible, we have posted travel planning files online.

TwiTips

Below is a list of our **Olympic Peninsula TwiTips** found online in the **TwiTips & Maps** directory for **Book One**.

TwiTips Important to *All* Twilighters Planning an Olympic Peninsula Twilight Saga Trip
http://www.TourTheTwilightSaga.com/B1/TwiTripPlanning.pdf

Selecting the Sites You Want to Visit
Deciding on the Dates of Your Trip
Determining How Long You'll Need for an Olympic Peninsula Twilight Saga Holiday
Preparation Important to Planning an Olympic Peninsula Visit
Olympic Peninsula Packing Plans

Info for International Twilighters
http://www.TourTheTwilightSaga.com/B1/InternationalTwilighters.pdf

Do You Need a US Visa to Visit Forks from a Foreign Country?
Passport Requirements for Foreign National Twilighters

Tour the Twilight Saga Book One

Olympic Peninsula Airport Options
http://www.TourTheTwilightSaga.com/B1/AirportOptions.pdf

Airport Options for Canadian Twilighters
Airport Options for *All* Twilighters: Fly to Seattle *or* Port Angeles
The Portland, Oregon Airport Option
Common Airport-to-Forks Drive Times

Olympic Peninsula Public Transportation Options
http://www.TourTheTwilightSaga.com/B1/PublicTransportation.pdf

Car Rental Twi Travel Tips
http://www.TourTheTwilightSaga.com/Tips/CarRental.pdf

Determining Your Rental Car Needs
Rental Car Insurance Info
GPS/SatNav Device Options
The Right-Side Driving Dilemma
Automatic Transmission Anxieties
How to Find the Best Rental Car Deals
Rental Car Check List to Use *Before* Leaving the Rental Car Lot
http://www.TourTheTwilightSaga.com/Tips/RentalCarCheckList.pdf

US Road Rules and Driving Details
http://www.TourTheTwilightSaga.com/B1/DrivingInTheUS.pdf

Are You Already Licensed to Drive in the Olympic Peninsula?
Do You Need an International Driving Permit?
US Driving Rules and Regulations
US Parking Practices
Automobile-Related US Terms with UK Translations

Twi Travel Tips

Twi Travel Tips contain information important to planning a Twilight Saga Tour *anywhere* in the world. You'll find a link to our Twi Travel Tips directory in the left navigation bar at the bottom of every *Tour the Twilight Saga* **webpage**.

Car Rental Tips
http://www.TourTheTwilightSaga.com/Tips/CarRental.pdf

Important Phone Info for Twication Planning and Traveling
http://www.TourTheTwilightSaga.com/Tips/PhoneNumbers.pdf

How to Dial Between Countries While Twilighting
US (and Canadian) Emergency and Universal Assistance Phone Numbers
Programming Your Phone with Contact Info for Your Nearest Embassy or Consulate

Telephones and Internet Access When Twilighting
http://www.TourTheTwilightSaga.com/Tips/PhoneInternet.pdf

Deciding What Phone to Use
Twilight Saga Site Time Zones
Options for Accessing the Internet

Packing Pointers
http://www.TourTheTwilightSaga.com/Tips/PackingPointers.pdf

A Collection of Universal Packing Pointers

Photography and Packing Pointers
http://www.TourTheTwilightSaga.com/Tips/Photography.pdf

Vital Photography Equipment and Where to Pack it
The Value of Bringing a *Spare* (Cheap) Digital Camera
Universal TwiPic-Taking Tips

Supplies to Purchase after Arrival
http://www.TourTheTwilightSaga.com/Tips/ShoppingList.pdf

Tour the Twilight Saga Book One

US Terminology Guide
http://www.TourTheTwilightSaga.com/Tips/USterminology.pdf

US English Terms Translated into UK English Terms
Floor Numbering in the US and Canada

1

Seattle, Washington

**Birthplace of Victoria's Newborn Army
Home of J. Jenks
The Twilight T-Shirt Trek**
http://en.wikipedia.org/wiki/Seattle
http://www.seattle.gov

Google Maps: 1st Avenue and Pike Street, Seattle, WA 98101

Visit Time: Plan on spending at least 2 hours at Pike Place Market, but don't be surprised if you stay far longer. T-shirt trekking Twilighters should schedule 1-2 hours in the Fremont area.

[Breaking Dawn Part 2 screenshot segment (enhanced)]

Tour the Twilight Saga Book One

Seattle is a coastal seaport city and the seat of King County, Washington. With an estimated population of 634,535 in 2012, Seattle is the largest city in the Pacific Northwest region of the U.S., and one of the fastest-growing cities in the country. Seattle is situated on a narrow strip of land sandwiched between Puget Sound—a Pacific Ocean inlet—and Lake Washington, approximately 100 miles (160 km) south of the U.S.-Canadian border. Closer to Asia and Alaska than any other major U.S. seaport, Port of Seattle is a premier gateway for products, cruise passengers and tourists, moving to and from North America.

[©2011 Jordon Kalilich] [©2010 Starbucks] [©2008 Walter Siegmund]

Best known for the **Space Needle**, **Starbucks'** corporate headquarters, and **Mount Rainier**, Seattle has a slew of other visitor attractions.
http://www.spaceneedle.com
http://www.seattle.gov/html/visitor/starbucks.htm
http://www.nps.gov/mora/index.htm

If visiting Seattle for more than the partial days of Twilight Saga Tour airport arrival and departure, be sure to explore non-Twilight Seattle travel resources. Start with the **Seattle.gov Visiting** page, where you'll learn about the city's:
- Points of Interest
- Things to Do
- Self-Guided Walking Tours
- Places to Stay, Eat, and Shop

http://www.seattle.gov/visiting/

Seattle.gov also has important visitor information, such as:
- Personal Safety Tips
- Guides to Public Transportation
- Tips for Touring the Region
- International Visitors' Info

Seattle—Site 1

Twilighters interested in seeing several of Seattle's most popular places should investigate the **Seattle CityPASS**—a booklet of tickets that admit you to six must-see Seattle attractions at any time within nine consecutive days after activation.

- **The Space Needle**: Each booklet has *two* tickets to the top, so you can enjoy the amazing daytime view as well as the sunset or city lights at night. The second ticket must be used within 24 hours of the first.
- **The Seattle Aquarium**
- **Argosy Cruises Harbor Tour**: A 1-hour, live-narrated cruise of Elliot Bay and Seattle Harbor, offering wonderful views of Seattle's skyline and waterfront, the Olympic and Cascade Mountains.
- **Pacific Science Center**
- **EMP Museum:** Formerly known as the Experience Music Project and Science Fiction Museum and Hall of Fame (EMP/SFM).
- **Woodland Park Zoo** *or* **Museum of Flight**

In 2013, the combined price of these tickets totaled $132.75 (£81) for Adults, $85.80 (£52) for Children ages 4 to 12 years-old. The 2013 CityPASS price: Adults $74 (£45), Children $49 (£30).

The CityPASS website is a great source of information for the attractions listed, even if you're not interested in buying a booklet.
http://www.citypass.com/seattle

In addition to the city's many points of interest, Seattle annually hosts several internationally known festivals, such as:
- The Northwest Folklife Festival that celebrates Pacific Northwest folk music and ethnic traditions. Held on Memorial Day weekend in May, it's the largest free festival of its kind in North America.
  http://www.nwfolklife.org/
- The 24-day **Seattle International Film Festival** in May and June.
  http://www.siff.net/
- June's **Seattle PrideFest**—one of the largest Gay Pride festivals in the United States.
  http://www.seattlepridefest.org
- The **Seafair Summer Festival:** This festival of maritime celebrations and competitions is officially held throughout June, July, and August. Additional Seafair-related events, however, are offered every month of the year.
  http://www.seafair.com/
  http://seattle.about.com/od/festivals/a/Seafair.htm

Tour the Twilight Saga Book One

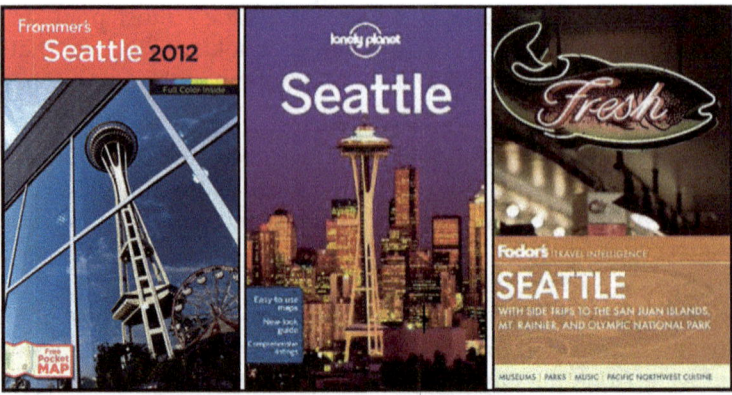

[© 2012 Frommer's] [©2014 Lonely Planet] [©2010 Fodor's]

Buying one or two of the non-Twilight Seattle travel guidebooks is a good idea if you'll be spending several days in Seattle. Before doing that, however, go to the **Frommer**'s Seattle webpage and peruse all the FREE information posted there.
http://www.frommers.com/destinations/seattle

COMPLETE GUIDE		Introduction
Introduction	Suggested Itineraries	
Planning a Trip	Maps	Frommer's Favorite Experiences
In Depth	Hotels	Best Dining Bets
Side Trips	Overview, more...	Best Hotel Bets
Organized Tours	Restaurants	
Walking Tours	Overview, more...	The Best Family Attractions
Active Pursuits	Attractions	The Best Offbeat Travel Experiences
Spectator Sports	Overview, more...	The Best Outdoor Pursuits
Shopping	Nightlife	
Overview, more...	Overview, more...	Best Free Things to Do

[Frommers.com screenshot segments (enhanced) above & below, ©2013 FrommerMedia LLC]

Above left is a master directory of Frommer's free Seattle information. Each heading leads to a subdirectory containing several pages of in-depth information. Above right is a list of the free-info pages found under the **Introduction** heading. Below is a list of free-info pages found under the **Planning a Trip** heading.

Seattle—Site 1

Planning a Trip		
Fast Facts	Money	Neighborhoods in Brief
	Getting Around	Tips for Families
Visitor Information	Entry Requirements & Customs	Tips for Gay and Lesbian Travelers
When to Go	Special-Interest Vacations	Tips for Senior Travelers
Calendar of Events	Sustainable Travel & Ecotourism	Tips for Travelers with Disabilities
Getting There	Orientation	Staying Connected

Tour the Twilight Saga authors promote the Frommer's Seattle travel guidebook precisely because Frommer's provides such a wealth of free information on its website. To look at other guides, search "Seattle travel guidebooks." Whatever guidebook you select, check for the newest available.

[*Eclipse* screenshot (enhanced)]

Seattle's Twilight Saga Sight

In *Eclipse*, Stephenie Meyer described a sudden rash of unsolved murders and disappearances occurring in Seattle—incidents eventually revealed as Victoria's efforts to create an army of newborns, led by her new partner, Riley Biers.

Tour the Twilight Saga Book One

[*Eclipse* screenshot segments (enhanced)]

Little explanation of Riley's background is found in the novel. We learn far more about him in the movie—something Stephenie collaborated on—including where he went missing.

> "Riley Biers was last seen at 16:15 (4:15pm) on Friday, May 21 2010, walking towards the Pike Place Market."

[©2013 CD Miller]

Pike Place Market
http://pikeplacemarket.org/
http://www.seattle.gov/neighborhoods/preservation/pikeplace.htm
http://en.wikipedia.org/wiki/Pike_Place_Market

Google Maps: Pike Place Market, Seattle, WA 98101
Or, 1st Avenue & Pike Street, Seattle, WA 98101.

Established in 1907, Seattle's **Pike Place Market** is one of the oldest continuously operating farmers markets in the United States, and the country's most historically authentic public market. Part of a nine-acre Market Historic District, Pike Place Market extends 3 blocks north of Pike Street to Virginia Street, and 2 blocks west from 1st Avenue to Western Avenue.

[©2013 CD Miller, above and below]

From the Pike Place Market website:

> "Pike Place Market's historic arcade, winding alleys, stairways and lower levels offer a multisensory experience of sights, sounds, tastes, aromas and textures. Taste what's in season at a farm stand. Listen to a Motown or bluegrass classic from buskers [street performers] while marveling over the creativity of the goods in the crafts market. Follow the scent of baking bread down the cobblestones to a European bakery. Peruse comics, collectibles, magic tricks, vinyl records, books and rare treasures in small shops. Take time to wander. The Market will amaze, delight and inspire you."

Tour the Twilight Saga Book One

[©2013 CD Miller]

Hours of Operation: Pike Place Market is open 362 days a year—closed only on Thanksgiving, Christmas, and New Year's Day. Operating hours vary for individual businesses.

- Bakeries and cafés begin opening as early as 6am
- The Pike Place Fish Market (where you'll find the famous fish-throwers) is open Monday-Saturday 6:30am to 6pm, Sunday 7am to 5pm
  https://www.pikeplacefish.com/
- Fresh produce and flower vendors begin opening at 7 or 8am
- The official market opening bell is sounded at 9am
- General merchant and crafter hours: 10am-6pm
- Last call for all Pike Place restaurants and bars: 1:30am

[©2013 CD Miller]

Seattle—Site 1

Your initial Pike Place Market destination should be the **Market Information** kiosk on Pike Street, between 1st Avenue and the giant clock sign perched above the arcade's main entrance. Open daily from 10am to 6pm, ask kiosk staff about the day's special events and pick up one of the two Market newspapers—they're free, and each has a business directory and **Market Map** on the back page. You'll need this map!

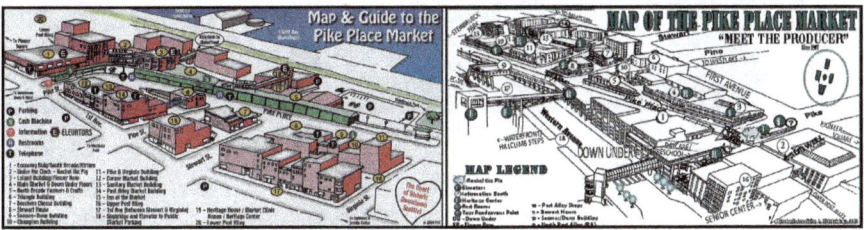

[Scanned image, ©2013 Pike Street Times] [PDF segment, ©2013 Pike Place Market News]

Pike Street Times is published quarterly—Spring, Summer, Fall, and Winter. **Pike Place Market News** is published monthly. Although both free newspapers are equally helpful, the Pike Street Times' map (above left) is visually easier to follow.

> **Please Note:** North is not *up* in either of these Market maps, and they're both skewed. Whatever map you're looking at, simply remember that the **Elliott Bay Waterfront** is WEST—seen at the top-right corner of the Pike Street Times map, at the bottom-left corner of the Pike Place Market News map.

https://www.facebook.com/pages/Pike-Street-Times/191065020911003
http://www.pikeplacemarketnews.com/

On both maps, a circled **question mark** indicates the Market Information kiosk's location. Browse the directory to determine what you're interested in seeing, circling each place's location on the map. Voila! You've just created a Pike Place Market itinerary to follow, *after* visiting the Twilight Saga site identified below.

If the Market Information kiosk is closed when you arrive, look around for one of the many black wire stands holding stacks of Market newspapers.

Tour the Twilight Saga Book One

[*Eclipse* screenshot (enhanced)]

At the beginning of *Eclipse*, Riley is seen being attacked by Victoria just after leaving a pub. These scenes were filmed in the **Gastown** area of **Vancouver, British Columbia** (TTTS Book Two). Filmmakers created and installed a neon sign to ensure that the movie's pub would be recognized as **The Pike Pub & Brewery** in Pike Place Market.

[©2013 CD Miller]

The Pike Pub & Brewery
http://www.pikebrewing.com/

Google Maps: 1415 1st Avenue, Seattle, WA 98101

Hours of Operation: Daily, 11am to Midnight. "Hoppy Hour" (discounted beer and appetizers) is offered Monday through Friday, from 4 to 6pm.

The Pike Pub & Brewery is a unique place to visit. The sitting area is centered around a multi-level brewery where brewers can be seen — in action — while you drink one of The Pike's handcrafted ales and dine on delicious pub grub. The Pike also houses a Microbrewery Museum and The Pike Company Store. Go to their website to learn more about this wonderful place.

Seattle—Site 1

The Pike Pub & Brewery is located in the **Economy Market** building.

- Pike Street Times map: The circled number 1 on the left side of the map.
- Pike Place Market News map: The circled number 2 on the right side of the map.

The Twilighter entrance (*Eclipse* neon sign) is on 1st Avenue, just around the corner from the Market Information kiosk, a few doors southeast of the First & Pike Newsstand.

[©2013 CD Miller]

Have your pic snapped beneath The Pike's neon sign on 1st Avenue, then enter the building's ground floor. Look to your left and you'll see a distinctive arch above the stairs leading down to The Pike Pub.

If visiting before the pub opens (11am), you'll find a chain across the stair entrance—as seen above right. Snap some pix at the arch, go elsewhere in the Market, and come back later if time allows. To visit The Pike Pub during lunch, Hoppy Hour(s), or dinner, it's best to have a reservation. **Reservations:** (206) 622-6044

> **Please Note:** Directions for **Going to Pike Place Market** follow the additional Seattle Twilight Saga info below.

Alas and Alack, there is *No* J. Jenks Site in Seattle

In the *Breaking Dawn* novel, Bella discovered Alice's secret message, drove to Seattle, and managed to find J. Jenks' office—a place that doesn't exist in the real-world.

After realizing what Alice and Jasper intended her to do, Bella commissioned Jenks to make counterfeit documents designed to help Jacob take Renesmee away and keep her safe from the Volturi. Jenks set a meeting for the documents' delivery.

> "Shall we meet at eight o'clock a week from tonight at The Pacifico? It's on Union Lake, and the food is exquisite."

Although there is a Lake Union in Seattle, there is no Pacifico restaurant.

[*Breaking Dawn* Part 2 screenshot (enhanced)]

Movie footage of Bella parking prior to her Pacifico restaurant meet with J. Jenks was filmed in **Vancouver, British Columbia** (TTTS Book Two).

[*Breaking Dawn* Part 2 screenshot (enhanced)]

Seattle—Site 1

Pacifico restaurant scenes were shot at a hotel restaurant in **New Orleans, Louisiana** (TTTS Book Four).

The Twilight T-Shirt Trek

Are you planning to collect Twilight Saga trip T-shirts and make a memory quilt similar to Bella's? If so, a special treat awaits you only a 15 minute drive from Pike Place Market—30 minutes by bus.

[*Eclipse* screenshot segment (enhanced)]

Of the 46 road trip T-shirts *Renée* (*Eclipse* movie props people) used to create Bella's memory quilt graduation gift, 37 are quite real, sporting logos designed by businesses or attractions that actually exist:

- 12 represent real-world Seattle businesses
- 7 are from places in Hawaii
- 12 are from places in California
- 6 are from sites in other US states

In 2009, when the quilt prop was being designed and constructed, 31 of the 37 real-world T-shirts were available from a single source: **Destee-Nation**, a Seattle-based T-shirt company that specializes in delightful and uniquely-U.S. road trip T-shirts.

> "Destee-Nation sells authentic T-shirts from landmark establishments and strives to preserve the rich neighborhood culture these places represent."

Tour the Twilight Saga Book One

[©2013 CD Miller]

In January 2014, 12 of *the Bella's* real-world road trip T-shirts were still available for purchase on Destee-Nation's website. Seattle-visiting Twilighters, however, can go to the shop and peruse them—and others—in person.

Please Note: Directions for traveling to Destee-Nation follow the **Going to Pike Place Market** section below.

[©2013 CD Miller]

Destee-Nation
http://www.desteenation.com/
https://www.facebook.com/pages/Destee-Nation-Shirt-Co/20984162203

Google Maps & SatNav/GPS: 3412 Evanston Ave N, Seattle, WA 98103

Whether or not you're looking for Bella and *Renée* road trip shirts, Destee-Nation's tiny shop is jam-packed full of fascinating—often hilarious—T-

Seattle—Site 1

shirts. Many preserve vintage logos no longer in use, and thus unavailable from the businesses they represent. Happily, each T-shirt's real-world business receives a tiny portion of the Destee-Nation sale price.

If the shop doesn't have your size in stock when you visit, Destee-Nation staff will order it and have it shipped to your home. If you're making a memory quilt, however, remember that the shirts don't have to fit! In fact, because small sizes are often cheaper, it's a good idea to buy small T-shirts for your quilt.

[*Eclipse* SF screenshot segments (enhanced)] [Bella Quilt Collage by CD Miller]

In an effort to justify the ridiculous number of hours she spent obsessing about *Renée* and Bella's road trip T-shirts, TTTS author CD Miller (Chas) created a PDF containing *all* the Bella graduation gift memory quilt information she managed to confirm. Twilighters planning to make a T-shirt memory quilt will find it illuminating. Twihards who want to visit Seattle businesses represented by a Bella road trip T-shirt (4 of which are in the Fremont neighborhood) *must* read the TTTS Bella's Quilt PDF.
http://www.TourTheTwilightSaga.com/B1/01BellasQuilt.pdf

As it happens, the Destee-Nation shop is located in a particularly visit-worthy area: Seattle's famous **Fremont** neighborhood.

Tour the Twilight Saga Book One

[PDF segment ©2013 Fremont.com] [©2013 CD Miller]

The Fremont Neighborhood
http://fremont.com/
http://www.fremontuniverse.com/
http://www.visitseattle.org/Visitors/Discover/Neighborhoods/Fremont.aspx
http://en.wikipedia.org/wiki/Fremont,_Seattle
http://www.sillyamerica.com/blog/2010/03/fremont-the-center-of-the-universe/

Seattle's Fremont neighborhood was so aptly described by **Val Bromann** — founder and head road tripper at Silly America dot com — we reproduced the following three paragraphs from her March of 2010 blog entry.

From Val Bromann:

Call it "The People's Republic of Fremont." Call it "The Artists' Republic of Fremont." Call it the "Center of the Universe." Whichever you choose, the Seattle neighborhood of Fremont is unlike anywhere you've ever been. A Mecca for any Silly American [or non-American] traveler, Fremont is covered from corner to corner with roadside attractions, weird statues, and pure wonderment. The community's unofficial slogan says it all: *De Libertas Quirkas* — "free to be peculiar."

Seattle—Site 1

[©2009 Val Bromann]

Locals believe that their little neighborhood is truly at the center of the universe, and who am I to argue? On a small median in the middle of the intersection where North 35th Street meets North 36th Street meets Fremont Avenue North—the place believed to be the true center point of the entire world—there is a tall wooden guidepost that will point you in the direction of almost anywhere you want to go, whether near or far.

[©2013 CD Miller]   [©2010 Alex of TunersandModels.com]

The Guidepost will help you find the local troll, or rocket, or Lenin statue [among many other street art exhibits]. It will also help you find more exotic destinations: the North Pole, Rio De Janeiro, Xanadu, Machu Picchu. Or, if you just stay put, you might just find your place at the center of the world. Thank you, Val!
http://en.wikipedia.org/wiki/Fremont_Troll
http://fremont.com/about/storyrocket-html/
http://en.wikipedia.org/wiki/Statue_of_Lenin,_Seattle

[©2012 The Artists Republic of Fremont]

Fremont Sunday Street Market
http://www.fremontmarket.com/
http://theartistsrepublicoffremont.wordpress.com/
https://www.facebook.com/FremontSundayMarket

Google Maps & SatNav/GPS: 3401 Evanston Ave N, Seattle, WA 98103
 [A 12 second walk from Destee-Nation!]

Hours of Operation: Sundays, 10am to 5pm

The Fremont Farmers Market and Craft Fair is a thriving and diverse European-style market that was established in 1990 and is open every Sunday of the year—rain or shine. Over 180 vendors and exhibitors delight visitors with everything imaginable, and some things that can't possibly be anticipated.

In addition to fresh produce and artisan food products, visitors find antiques, vintage and modern fashions, estate sale treasures, world imports, as well as works created by local artists and craftspeople.

> **Please Note:** All Fremont neighborhood street-side parking spaces are free on Sundays, as are many of its car parks. If you want to avoid crowds when visiting Destee-Nation and the Fremont neighborhood, however, **do not journey here on a Sunday**—either by car or public transport.

Seattle—Site 1

Going to Pike Place Market
http://www.pikeplacemarket.org/pages/directions-parking

Google Maps: 1st Avenue and Pike Street, Seattle, WA 98101

Being such a large metropolitan area, Seattle can be somewhat complicated to navigate. We've done our best to streamline the following transportation tips and directions. Unfortunately, they still ain't short.

[Internet-posted image segment (enhanced), ©2010 Adam Dachis]

🚍 Pike Place Market via Public Transport

Six separate transit providers operate public transportation options in the Seattle-Tacoma metropolitan area—*not* counting the Washington State Ferries. Happily, Twilighters need only become acquainted with Seattle's two primary transport authorities.

    King County Metro Transit runs all of the city's Metro Busses, its small fleet of Seattle Street Cars, and a Water Taxi service that crosses Elliot Bay between Pier 50 in downtown Seattle and Seacrest Park Dock in Western Seattle.
http://metro.kingcounty.gov/
http://en.wikipedia.org/wiki/Transportation_in_Seattle#Mass_transit
http://www.seattlestreetcar.org/
http://en.wikipedia.org/wiki/Seattle_Streetcar_Network
http://www.kingcounty.gov/transportation/kcdot/WaterTaxi.aspx

    Sound Transit is the regional transportation authority and operates an extensive system of express buses, light rail trains, and commuter trains within the Central Puget Sound area.
http://www.soundtransit.org/

Tour the Twilight Saga Book One

If you'll be using public transportation for two or more days, go to the independent **Seattle Transit Blog** website to learn important tips for getting around the city and read a preview of the **ORCA** card.
http://seattletransitblog.com/seattle-for-visitors/

The ORCA card is accepted for Washington State Ferries, and all Seattle modes of transportation run by King County Metro Transit and Sound Transit authorities.
https://www.orcacard.com

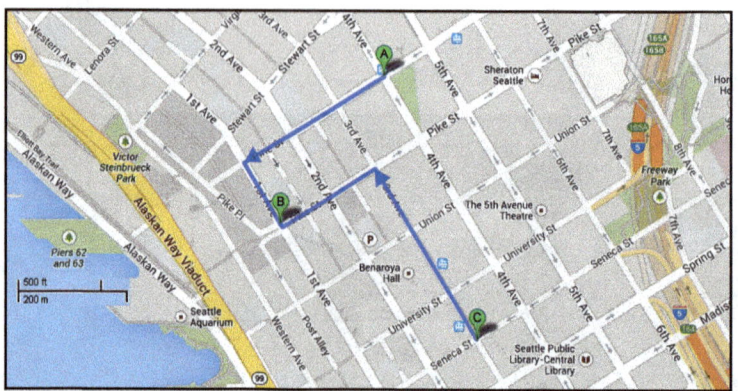

[Google Maps segments married & enhanced, ©2013 Google]

Twilighters traveling to Pike Place Market from the Seattle-Tacoma International Airport (Sea-Tac) can ride the **Sound Transit Link Light Rail** to either of two rail stations near Pike Place Market. As seen in the map thumbnail above, **Westlake Station (A)** is 4 blocks from the Market Information kiosk **(B)** at 1st and Pike Street. **University Street Station (C)** is 5 blocks from the kiosk.
http://www.soundtransit.org/Trip-Planner

> **Please Note:** Signs seen inside the airport are rumored to be rather confusing when seeking the departure point for Seattle-bound busses and trains. If you're unsure which way to walk, ask for directions from a uniformed airport information volunteer (blue blazer) or security officer.

Seattle—Site 1

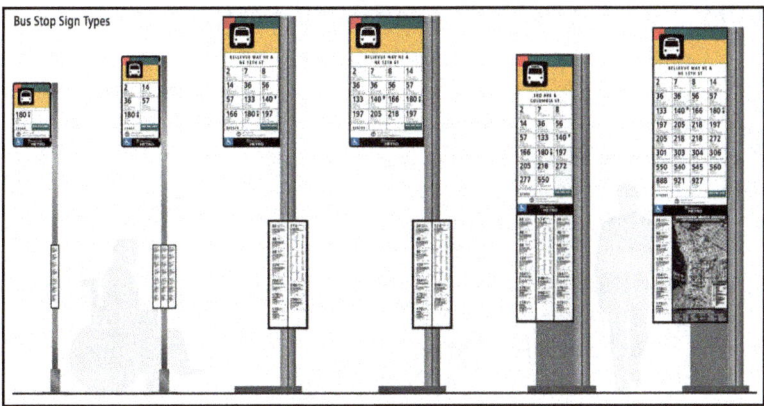

[©2011 Seattle Transit Blog]

Twilighters traveling to Pike Place Market from anywhere within Seattle can ride a **King County Metro Transit Bus**. Plan your bus trip online by visiting the link below. Or, simply go to the nearest bus stop and ask the first-arriving bus driver for instructions.
http://tripplanner.kingcounty.gov/

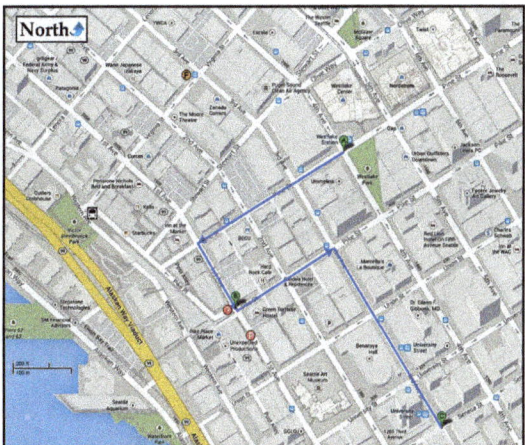

[Google Maps segments married & enhanced, ©2013 Google]
http://www.TourTheTwilightSaga.com/B1/01PublicTransMap.pdf

To assist Twilighters using public transportation, we created a map showing the location of Pike Place Market's Light Rail Stations and Bus Stops (a full-sized version of the thumbnail image above).

29

Tour the Twilight Saga Book One

Pike Place Market Public Transportation Map Key:

- **A: Westlake Station;** 4th Ave and Pine St., Seattle, WA
- **B: Market Information kiosk** (accompanied by a Red-Circled question mark); 1st Avenue and Pike Street, Seattle, WA 98101
- **C: University Street Station;** 3rd Ave and Seneca St., Seattle, WA
- **Big Black Bus Icon:** The covered Pike Place Market Metro Bus stop on a Virginia Street island between Western Avenue and Pike Place.
- **Little Blue Bus Icons:** Several uncovered Metro Bus stop locations found on surrounding streets.
- **Orange-Circled F:** The 3rd Avenue and Virginia Street bus stop for Metro Busses heading to the Fremont neighborhood.
- **Red-Circled P:** The Pike Pub & Brewery Twilighter entrance, 1415 1st Avenue, Seattle, WA 98101

[©2012 William Bird]

Twilighters planning to visit the Seattle Space Needle before or after Pike Place Market will enjoy riding the famous Seattle Center Monorail.

Hours of Operation: Opens at 7:30am Monday-Friday, 8:30am on Saturday and Sunday. Closes at 9pm Sunday-Thursday, 11pm on Friday and Saturday. Closed on Thanksgiving Day and Christmas Day.
http://www.seattlemonorail.com/

The Seattle Center Monorail departs every 10 minutes from two stations: the downtown Westlake Center Station (5th Avenue and Pine Street—5 blocks from the Market Information kiosk) and the Seattle Center Station at the Space Needle. The ride is non-stop and lasts approximately 2 minutes.

Monorail tickets are one-way and must be purchased onsite—cash only. In 2013, the Adult monorail fare was $2.25 (£1.37). The Youth and Senior monorail fare (ages 5-12 and 65+) was $1 (£0.60).

Twilighters driving to downtown Seattle can park at Pike Place Market and ride the monorail to and from the Space Needle.

[©2013 CD Miller]

🚗 Driving to Pike Place Market

Seattle's extremely congested roadways can be challenging even for those accustomed to driving in the U.S. Twilighters who prefer to avoid hazarding Seattle's traffic by parking outside the downtown area and riding in on a bus should visit the **King County Park & Ride** webpage. There you can find the Park & Ride location most convenient to your Seattle lodgings, or the direction from which you'll be driving to Seattle.
http://metro.kingcounty.gov/tops/parknride/parknride.html

If renting a car at Sea-Tac airport, the **Burien Transit Center Park & Ride** garage is only 4 miles away and you'll not need to travel the infamously-congested I-5 to reach it. A bus ride between Burien Transit Center and Pike Place Market ranges between 30 and 60 minutes, depending on the time of day and traffic conditions—the same amount of time associated with driving downtown from Sea-Tac. The address posted for Burien Transit Center (14900 4th Avenue Southwest, Burien, WA) can be problematic. Instead, use the car park entrance coordinates below.

SatNav/GPS Entrance Coordinates: 47.469568,-122.338869
http://metro.kingcounty.gov/tops/parknride/m_burientcboarding.html
http://metro.kingcounty.gov/tops/parknride/pr-south-seattle.html

Tour the Twilight Saga Book One

[Street view image segment (enhanced), ©July, 2011 Google]

Twilighters happy to brave the drive to Pike Place Market should note that, although the Market's streets are open to vehicle traffic, they're often swarmed with pedestrians—making it tricky and time-consuming to safely navigate them in a car. Rather than driving to the Market's address, program your SatNav/GPS device for one of the nearby Western Avenue car parks.

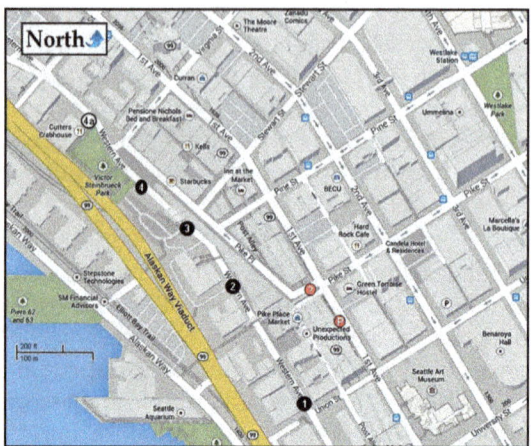

[Google Maps segments married & enhanced, ©2013 Google]
http://www.TourTheTwilightSaga.com/B1/01DrivingMaps.pdf

To assist driving Twilighters, we created a map identifying the four Western Avenue car parks closest to Pike Place Market (a full-sized version of the thumbnail image above), as well as maps showing the most direct routes to Western Avenue from the I-5 exits closest to the Market—one for those approaching from Sea-Tac (the south), one approaching from the north.

Seattle—Site 1

Please Note: Our Western Avenue route maps are intended as references to acquaint Twilighters with the area prior to travel. Traffic and road conditions at the time of actual travel may require alternate routing. Trust your SatNav/GPS device.

Pike Place Market Driving Maps Key

Car park addresses do not always lead you to the car park entrances. Program your SatNav/GPS with the Entrance Coordinates for car park **1** if approaching from the south, garage **4** if approaching from the north.

1: **Market Place Republic Parking Car Park**
   Address: 1301 Western Avenue, Seattle, WA 98101
   Entrance Coordinates: 47.607501,-122.34036
   Hours: Unknown—though likely the same as the Market Place garage **(4)**, below.

2: **Pike Place Market Car Park**
   Address: 1531 Western Avenue, Seattle, WA 98101
   Entrance Coordinates: 47.608789,-122.34166
   Hours: 5am to 2am, daily
   Pike Place Market's website describes this lot as being: "the most convenient and affordable option for parking at Pike Place Market. ... easy access to the Market via elevator and sky bridge."
   http://www.pikeplacemarket.org/pages/public-market-garage

3: **Pike Place Market Desimone Car Park**
   Address: 1615 Western Avenue, Seattle, WA 98101
   Entrance Coordinates: 47.60949,-122.342359
   Hours: 5am to 2am, daily
   Although there's no elevator or sky bridge from here to the Market, this lot is still extremely convenient and affordable.

4: **Market Place Republic Parking Garage**
   Address: 1615 Western Avenue, Seattle, WA 98121
   Entrance Coordinates: 47.610016,-122.343288
   Hours: Mon-Thurs, 5:30am-12:30am ... Fri, 5:30am-1:30am ... Sat, 6:45am-1:30am ... Sun, 8am-11:30pm
   This underground parking garage has 3 levels and lies beneath Victor Steinbrueck Park. If you park on the first level below ground, you can walk out of the garage via a stairway next to the Western Avenue vehicle in-ramp—the point closest to Pike Place Market. You cannot walk back *into* the garage via that stairway.

4a: When returning to your car, here is where you'll find the pedestrian entrance to all levels of the Market Place Republic Parking Garage.

Tour the Twilight Saga Book One

Red-Circled Question Mark: The Market Information kiosk
1st Avenue and Pike Street, Seattle, WA 98101

Red-Circled P: The Pike Pub & Brewery Twilighter entrance,
1415 1st Avenue, Seattle, WA 98101

Seattle.gov has an **e-Park** webpage that provides a live feed of parking spaces available at Downtown Seattle garages. If you've got a smart phone, go there and bookmark it.
http://www.seattle.gov/transportation/epark/mobile/default.htm

[©2013 CD Miller]

Fees at the two Pike Place Market car parks (above left and center) are far less expensive than those at the Republic Parking Market Place car park or garage (above right). The earlier you arrive, the more likely you'll find space in the cheaper lots.

If you arrive before 9:30am, Pike Place Market lots also offer a discounted **Early Bird Special** fee [$10 (£6) in 2013], good for up to 10 hours. An **Evening Special** discount [$7 (£4.25)] is available if you arrive after 5pm, and is good until the car park closes at 2am — up to 9 hours.

If you arrive too late for the Early Bird Special and too early for the Evening Special, alternative discounts may be available. Ask the Pike Place Market lot attendant to validate your ticket and give you a free hour of parking. If you purchase anything within the Market, present your car park ticket to the merchant. You may receive another free hour of parking. If you dine at a Pike Place Market restaurant in the evening, the restaurant may validate your ticket so that parking is *free* after 5pm.

Seattle—Site 1

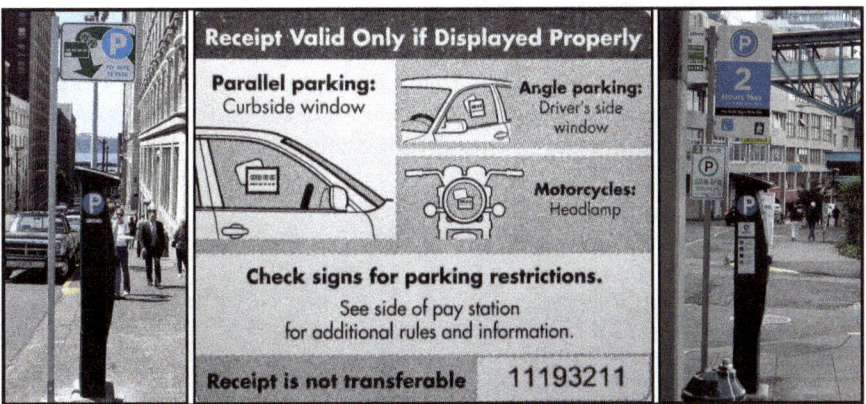

[©2013 CD Miller]

Street parking spaces are available on many streets in the Pike Place Market area, including 1st Avenue and Western Avenue. Although these spaces are free after 8pm—and free all day on Sundays—when parking at any other times you must purchase a pay and display ticket at the block's parking pay station. And, you may be limited to only 2 hours of parking.

Yes, at the beginning of this chapter we said that Pike Place Market could be visited in only 2 hours. Parking at a space *limited* to 2 hours, however, will likely invoke Murphy's Law—guaranteeing that something in the Market will make you want to stay longer. Park in a car park.

> **Please Note:** If you park on the street anywhere in Seattle, be very sure to properly display your parking receipt. (See the central image above.) Improper parking receipt display fines are steep [$29 (£18) in 2013]. Seattle parking authorities will use your car's license plate info to find you—rental or not—long after you've returned home.

Going to Destee-Nation and the Fremont Neighborhood

Google Maps & SatNav/GPS: 3412 Evanston Ave N, Seattle, WA 98103

Before heading to Fremont via any mode of transportation, download the free **Fremont Walking Guide** to your tablet or smart phone—or print and pack it. The link is usually found in the left nav-bar of Fremont.com pages.
http://fremont.com/

Tour the Twilight Saga Book One

Many Fremont neighborhood businesses distribute copies of the free guide, but it's best to have it with you when you first arrive. Why? The Fremont Walking Guide includes a map to all the fabu Fremont neighborhood sites you can visit before and after the Destee-Nation shop. Without the map, you may have to back-track to see things you'd know to visit had you had it with you to begin with.

[Internet-posted image segment (enhanced), ©Christopher MacKechnie]

Destee-Nation-Fremont Neighborhood via Public Transport

Twilighters with smart phones can bookmark the King County Trip-Planner and plot a bus trip to the Fremont neighborhood when ready to leave Pike Place Market.
http://tripplanner.kingcounty.gov/

Twilighters without smart phones can simply walk to the **3rd Avenue and Virginia Street Metro Bus stop** (the orange-circled **F** on our Pike Place Market Public Transportation Map), and board the next bus to Fremont. Three Metro busses travel between this bus stop and the Fremont neighborhood.
- 26 East Green Lake [Return bus: 26 Downtown Seattle]
- 28 Whittier Heights [Return bus: 28 Downtown Seattle]
- 40 North Gate [Return bus: 40 Downtown Seattle]

Disembark the bus at **Fremont Avenue North and North 34th Street**. From there, walk one block west on North 34th Street to Evanston Avenue North. Turn right and walk one block north. You'll see the Destee-Nation shop on your right.

After your Destee-Nation visit, use the Fremont Walking Guide to wander the neighborhood. When ready to return to Pike Place Market—or your Seattle area lodgings—walk back to the bus stop at Fremont Avenue North and North 34th Street.

Seattle—Site 1

[©2013 CD Miller]

🚗 Driving to Destee-Nation and the Fremont Neighborhood

Google Maps & SatNav/GPS: 3412 Evanston Ave N, Seattle, WA 98103

TTTS authors suggest using the Destee-Nation address (above) to program your SatNav/GPS, and driving by the shop to orient yourself prior to seeking a space.

[©2013 CD Miller]

If you use a 2-hour street parking space when visiting Destee-Nation and the Fremont neighborhood, be alert for "back-in angle parking" rules, in addition to being sure you properly display the street parking receipt purchased from the pay station.

Tour the Twilight Saga Book One

[Street view image segments (enhanced)—above and below—©2011 Google]

Twilighters interested in enjoying Seattle's famous Fremont neighborhood for more than 2 hours should park in one of the area's several car parks and garages. We suggest that you simply drive around the area watching for Public Parking signs. Alternatively, you can go to the Fremont car park website to explore them ahead of time and use a specific car park's address to program your SatNav/GPS.
http://www.u-parksystem.com/locations/default.asp#fremont_seattle

🛏 Lodging in Seattle, Washington

When looking for lodgings in any major metropolitan area, your best bet is to stay at a place recommended by a friend or associate. In the absence of a personal recommendation, get ready to do some research.

First, however, do *not* simply search for the type of Seattle accommodation you're interested in. While that method works fine for finding a place to stay in small communities such as Port Angeles or Forks, large cities yield far too many options to be reasonably investigated. Additionally, photos or descriptions of an accommodation posted online by the business owner may be different from its real-world appearance and quality.

Seattle—Site 1

Use TripAdvisor to Search for Seattle Lodgings
http://www.tripadvisor.com/Hotels-g60878-Seattle_Washington-Hotels.html

Peruse Seattle Hotels, or click on the Best Value box link to look at Seattle Motels. Or, switch to one of the other tab links to investigate B&Bs and Inns, Specialty Lodgings (including Hostels), Vacation Rentals, or Special Offers. You'll still need to sift through several descriptions and reviews, but this method is far less arduous than using an Internet search engine.

Consider Staying at a Sea-Tac Airport Area Hotel

When only lodging in Seattle on the night (or two) before your flight home, the most convenient place to stay is near the Sea-Tac Airport **Rental Car Return Lot**—a lot used by *all* airport car rental agencies. When ready to check in for your flight, drive a few minutes to the return lot, turn in your car, and board the free airport shuttle.
http://www.portseattle.org/Sea-Tac/Maps-and-Directions/Pages/Rental-Car-Facility.aspx

Google Maps & SatNav/GPS: 3150 South 160th Street, Seattle, WA 98188

Happily, there are plenty of hotels near Sea-Tac to choose from.
http://www.tripadvisor.com/Hotels-g58732-SeaTac_Washington-Hotels.html

Of the 34 airport area hotels listed by TripAdvisor, below are the 13 located closest to the Sea-Tac rental car return lot.

- **Red Roof Inn Seattle Airport – SEATAC**, 2 stars, less than a mile from the rental car return lot
- **Holiday Inn Seattle Airport**, 3 stars, 1 mile away
- **Hilton Seattle Airport & Conference Center**, 3.5 stars, 1.1 miles away
- **Seattle Airport Marriott**, 3.5 stars, 1.3 miles away
- **Radisson Hotel Seattle Airport**, 3.5 stars, 1.4 miles away
- **Red Lion Hotel Seattle Airport**, 3 stars, 1.5 miles away
- **Doubletree by Hilton Seattle Airport**, 3.5 stars, 1.7 miles away
- **Coast Gateway Hotel**, 3 stars, 2 miles away
- **La Quinta Inn & Suites Seattle Sea-Tac**, 2.5 stars, 2 miles away
- **Hampton Inn and Suites Seattle-Airport/28th Ave**, 2.5 stars, 2.1 miles away
- **Super 8 Seattle**, 2 stars, 2.1 miles away
- **Quality Inn Sea-Tac Airport** (formerly Travelodge), 2 stars, 2.1 miles away
- **Days Inn Seattle/Sea-Tac International Airport**, 2 stars, 2.2 miles away

Tour the Twilight Saga Book One

Grocery and Starbucks near Sea-Tac

The distances above also reflect each hotel's proximity to a gigantic **Safeway Grocery Store**. (UK Twilighters: think Tesco Superstore.) This Safeway's many specialty sections include a Wells Fargo Bank, Starbucks Coffee shop, Pharmacy, Sushi Bar, Pizzeria, Liquor store, Bakery, and Deli. Although specialty sections have specific hours, the bulk of this grocery store is open 24 hours a day, 7 days a week.
http://local.safeway.com/wa/seattle-1493.html
http://www.starbucks.com/store/12621/us/safeway-seattle-1493/4011-s-164th-seattle-wa-981883067

Google Maps & SatNav/GPS: 4011 South 164th, Seattle, WA 98188

Sea-Tac Area Motel Suggestion

Twilighters looking to book the cheapest possible accommodation near the Sea-Tac rental car return lot should review our **Bargain Basement Sea-Tac Motel** supplement.
http://www.TourTheTwilightSaga.com/B1/01BargainMotel.pdf

2

Port Angeles, Washington

Novel Locations-Bella and Edward's First Date Restaurant
http://www.cityofpa.us/
http://en.wikipedia.org/wiki/Port_Angeles,_Washington
http://twilightsaga.wikia.com/wiki/Port_Angeles,_Washington

Google Maps & SatNav/GPS: 118 East 1st Street, Port Angeles, WA 98362

Visit Time: Plan no less than 2.5 hours to enjoy your Bella's Mushroom Ravioli dinner reservation and snap pix at other nearby Port Angeles novel locations.

○✥○

Forks lies within Clallam County, about an hour's drive southeast of **Port Angeles**, the Clallam County seat. Forks doesn't have a movie theater or any major department stores. Real-world Forks teenagers have to drive to Port Angeles if they want to do some serious shopping or enjoy a movie date. An accomplished researcher, Stephenie Meyer wrote a few Bella-trips to Port Angeles in *Twilight* and *New Moon*.

Rather than make Charlie drive 7 hours (3½ hours each way) to pick his daughter up at the **Seattle-Tacoma International Airport**, Stephenie had Bella fly into Port Angeles' tiny **William R. Fairchild International Airport** when she moved back to Forks.

Tour the Twilight Saga Book One

> "It's a four-hour flight from Phoenix to Seattle, another hour in a small plane up to Port Angeles, and then an hour drive back down to Forks."

Twilight Saga Sites in Port Angeles

We've listed the six Port Angeles Twilight Saga novel sites in order of most-Twilicious to least-Twilicious. Happily, the first five are found in the small Port Angeles downtown area within easy walking distance of each other.

[©2013 Tara Miller]

☺Bella Italia Restaurant
http://www.bellaitaliapa.com/
https://www.facebook.com/BellaItaliaPA

Google Maps & SatNav/GPS: 118 East 1st Street, Port Angeles, WA 98362

Hours of Operation: Open 7 days a week, after 4pm.

Film Site: St Helens, Oregon, TTTS Book Three

Stephenie Meyer based the name of Bella and Edward's first date restaurant—"La Bella Italia"—on the real-world **Bella Italia** restaurant in Port Angeles. According to *Twilight in Forks* footage, Stephenie phoned Bella Italia to discover their menu items during her research, and spoke with Brett Lowe, the restaurant's manager at that time.

> "[Stephenie] had some ideas about the meals she wanted her characters to have at our restaurant, and began by asking whether we featured gnocchi on the menu."

Brett explained that they no longer served gnocchi (potato dumplings), due to lack of popularity. Next, she asked whether they offered veal scaloppini.

Port Angeles—Site 2

After Brett described their scaloppini-similar dishes, none were what she was looking for. Finally, Stephenie asked if Bella Italia served a mushroom ravioli entrée. *BINGO!*

[©2013 Tara Miller]

Bella Italia's menu fluctuates throughout the year, because their signature dishes are based on the seasonal availability of fresh, local produce. Prior to the Twilight Saga popularity explosion, their mushroom ravioli entrée was offered only during the fall mushroom season. Today, however, "Bella's Mushroom Ravioli in creamy besciamella with Olympic forest mushrooms" is available year-round. Take it from us, this dish is divinely delicious—even if you're not a Twilighter!

Plan your Bella Italia visit date based on your airport's location and flight arrival/departure times.

- Will you reach Port Angeles between 4 and 9pm when driving to Forks from your arrival airport?
- Will you reach Port Angeles between 4 and 9pm during your drive back to the airport on the night before your departure flight?
- Or, is it more convenient to schedule a return trip between Forks and Port Angeles while lodging in the Forks area?

Immediately after deciding your Bella Italia visit date, make a dinner reservation, but *don't* do it on their website. You cannot reserve a table via the Internet more than a couple months in advance. More importantly— for Twi-Couples—you cannot reserve the restaurant's designated **Edward**

Tour the Twilight Saga Book One

& Bella Table when booking online. Instead, make your Bella Italia dinner reservation as far in advance as possible by calling the restaurant between 7 and 9pm (after the dinner rush, Pacific Standard Time) and speaking to a live person. **(360) 457-5442.**

[Facebook-posted photo segment (enhanced), ©2011 Bella Italia]

Bella Italia is a beautiful restaurant, but it looks *nothing* like the novel's restaurant description or the movie's set. Granted, Stephenie wrote very little about what the restaurant's interior looked like in the novel.

> "'Perhaps something more private?' he insisted quietly to the host. ... She turned and led us around a partition to a small ring of booths—all of them empty."

But, because she collaborated on *Twilight* set designs, it is reasonable to surmise that the "Bloated Toad" set seen on screen represents the author's personal vision of La Bella Italia's interior.

Please Note: We suspect that the movie's restaurant was called the Bloated Toad because of licensing difficulties related to the fact that real-world "La Bella Italia" restaurants exist in Virginia Beach, Virginia (U.S.A.), as well as in Wellington, New Zealand.

Thanks to **TwiFoot Tours'** Rosemary Colandrea (Site #12), we learned that there *is* a Port Angeles restaurant with a seating layout and ambience similar to La Bella Italia descriptions *and* the Bloated Toad's interior set. Oddly enough, that restaurant is directly across the street from Bella Italia: **Michael's Seafood and Steakhouse.**

Port Angeles—Site 2

[©2013 Tara Miller]

☺Michael's Seafood and Steakhouse
http://www.michaelsdining.com/
https://www.facebook.com/MichaelsPA

Google Maps & SatNav/GPS: 117 B East 1st Street, Port Angeles WA, 98363

Hours of Operation: Open Sunday through Wednesday, 4pm to 10pm; 4pm to 11pm on Thursday through Saturday.

Call the restaurant between 7 and 9pm (after the dinner rush, Pacific Standard Time) to make your reservation well in advance. **(360) 417-6929.**

A mid-block pedestrian crosswalk stretches across East 1st Street between Bella Italia's front door and Michael's front door. After entering Michael's, walk down the stairs and turn to the right. There you'll find the private booths Stephenie described in the novel.

[©2013 Carol & Matt Hutchison]

Tour the Twilight Saga Book One

While lodging in Forks during their 2013 visit, Twilighters Carol and Matt of Arkansas made a return-trip to Port Angeles and thoroughly enjoyed Michael's cozy, romantic ambiance—as well as the food. Compare Matt and Carol's *Emmett and Rosalie* date night photo above with the *Twilight* screenshot below. The interior of Michael's looks far more like the Bloated Toad than Bella Italia does.

[*Twilight* screenshot (enhanced)]

Tour the Twilight Saga Suggestions:

- You *must* schedule one night to dine at Bella Italia during your Olympic Peninsula Twilight Saga tour so you can enjoy Bella's mushroom ravioli.
- If flying into and out of the William R. Fairchild International Airport and lodging at least one night in Port Angeles, you can easily dine at both Bella Italia and Michael's restaurants by making only *one* return-trip here from Forks.
- If you'll not be arriving via Port Angeles' little airport, but have 3 or more days in the Forks/La Push area, consider scheduling return-trips between Forks and Port Angeles on *two* nights: one to dine at Bella Italia, one to dine at Michael's. It's only an hour's drive each way, and the scenery is absolutely gorgeous—especially the 8 miles of Hwy 101 that wind along the southern shore of **Lake Crescent**.

http://www.nps.gov/olym/planyourvisit/visiting-lake-crescent.htm
http://en.wikipedia.org/wiki/Lake_Crescent

Port Angeles—Site 2

[©2013 Tara Miller]

☻The Lincoln Theatre
http://www.facebook.com/pages/Lincoln-Theatre/100914153286488

Google Maps & SatNav/GPS: 132 East 1st Street, Port Angeles, WA, 98362

Film Site: Paramount Theatre, Vancouver, British Columbia, TTTS Book Two.

Early in *New Moon* Bella became crippled by the loss of Edward and withdrew into a self-imposed isolation for several months. Charlie finally became so worried that he threatened to send her to live with her mother in Florida. To appease her father and remain in Forks, Bella swore to resume a more social behavior.

> "I'll make plans with Jessica, … We'll go to Port Angeles and watch a movie."

Bella honored her promise by getting Jess to go with her to a movie in Port Angeles. Later in *New Moon* (both novel and film), Bella made another trip to the same movie theater with Jacob and Mike.

Port Angeles has two movie theaters. The **Lincoln Theatre**, however, is the only one with a façade architecturally similar to the Vancouver, BC, theatre used to film all *New Moon* exterior Port Angeles movie theater scenes. Best of all, it's practically next door to Bella Italia.

After enjoying your meal at Bella Italia (or Michael's), walk southwest on East 1st Street, almost to Lincoln Street. There you can snap Lincoln Theatre pix when its marquee is lighted, and can closely recreate the *New Moon* screenshots seen below.

[*New Moon* screenshots (enhanced), above and below]

The Port Angeles Dazzled by Twilight Store

Address: 135 East 1st Street, Port Angeles, WA 98362

Both Bing and Google Maps incorrectly indicate this address' location—see our real-world location info below.

Hours of Operation: Closed since 2011.

The Port Angeles **Dazzled by Twilight** (DBT) store no longer exists, and thus is *not* a Tour the Twilight Saga site. We mention it only because some Twilighters have heard it was here and may be interested in the DBT story.

Port Angeles—Site 2

[Port Angeles DBT, ©2010 PietrosMomma]

In 2009, Annette Root—owner of the Forks DBT store—opened a second DBT store in Port Angeles. It was located across the street from the Lincoln Theatre, on the northwest corner of the East 1st Street and Lincoln Street intersection, in the ground floor of the **Port Angeles Elks Naval Lodge** building.

The Port Angeles DBT store was abruptly closed in December of 2011. Two months later, the Elks auctioned off boxes and boxes of DBT merchandise—at dirt-cheap prices—in an attempt to recoup the almost $4000 in back rent and utilities that Ms. Root owed.

Twilighters interested in learning the full story of DBT's rapid rise to fame, and equally rapid demise, can read about it in the PDF we created.
http://www.TourTheTwilightSaga.com/B1/DBTstory.pdf

After snapping your Lincoln Theater pix, look across the street and "salute"—in whatever manner you deem appropriate—the site that once housed the Port Angeles Dazzled by Twilight store.

[©2013 CD Miller]

Tour the Twilight Saga Book One

😠Port Book and News
http://www.portbooknews.com/
http://portangelesdowntown.com/port_book_and_news.php

Google Maps & SatNav/GPS: 104 East 1st Street, Port Angeles, WA 98362

Hours of Operation: Monday through Saturday, 8am-7pm; 9am-5pm on Sunday.

Film Site: St Helens, Oregon, TTTS Book Three.

After doing her best to participate in prom dress shopping, Bella left to look for a bookstore, promising to meet Jess and Angela in an hour, at the restaurant where they planned to eat before heading home.

> "I had no trouble finding the bookstore, but it wasn't what I was looking for. The windows were full of crystals, dream-catchers, and books about spiritual healing. I didn't even go inside."

No bookstore in Port Angeles fits the novel's description, or looks anything like the movie's film site and interior set. Only a couple doors northwest of Bella Italia, however, **Port Book and News** is perfect for Twilighters seeking to snap pix in front of a Port Angeles bookstore. If you have time before your dinner reservation, go inside and browse their small selection of books about the Quileute people.

[*Twilight* screenshot (enhanced)]

Port Angeles—Site 2

☹Gottschalks Department Store
http://en.wikipedia.org/wiki/Gottschalks

Google Maps & SatNav/GPS: 200 West 1st Street, Port Angeles, WA 98362

Film Site: St Helens, Oregon, TTTS Book Three.

In *Twilight*, Bella accompanied Jessica and Angela to "the one big department store" in Port Angeles. When Stephenie was writing *Twilight*, **Gottschalks** was that store. Unfortunately, the Fresno, California-based company went bankrupt in 2009, and all 58 Gottschalks department stores were closed.

In July of 2011, the abandoned Port Angeles Gottschalks building was purchased by a locally-owned business that had outgrown its original location. After extensive renovation and redesign, the new **Country Aire Natural Food Market** opened a year later.
http://www.countryairemarket.com

Only a 4 minute walk northwest of the Bella Italia Restaurant, Twihards can visit the old Gottschalks department store building. Be warned, however, it no longer looks *anything* like a place where someone would shop for prom dresses.

☹The Port Angeles McDonalds

Google Maps & SatNav/GPS: 1706 East Front Street, Port Angeles, WA 98362

Film Site: This novel event didn't appear on screen.

In *New Moon*, after she and Jessica left the Port Angeles movie theater, Bella found herself oddly drawn to some dangerous-looking men loitering outside a nearby bar—One Eyed Pete's. While approaching them, Bella experienced the first episode of seeing and hearing Edward psychically. After rejoining Jessica (who was thoroughly disgusted with Bella's reckless behavior), the two girls walked to the Port Angeles McDonalds and ate dinner.

> "I'd bet that [Jessica] was wishing we'd taken her car instead of walking the short distance from the theater, so that she could use the drive-through."

The only **McDonald's** in Port Angeles is 1.6 miles southeast of Bella Italia—a 35 minute walk, one-way. Since this novel activity didn't appear on screen, consider simply hitting the Port Angeles McDonald's drive-through to purchase a beverage and/or snack before heading to your next destination.

Nonexistent Port Angeles Twilight Saga Sites

[*Twilight* screenshot (enhanced)]

After leaving the "Thunderbird and Whale" bookstore in *Twilight*, Bella walked through an alley behind it where she was stalked by four men. Happily, Edward came to her rescue in the nick of time.

Because this is an entirely fictional book store, there is little point in wandering around real-world Port Angeles back alleys. Additionally, this segment of the novel was filmed in a place that *can* be visited: **St Helens, Oregon, TTTS Book Three**.

[*New Moon* screenshot (enhanced)]

Yet another entirely fictional Port Angeles novel site, One Eyed Pete's is a bar that doesn't exist anywhere in the real world. *New Moon* One Eyed Pete's scenes—including Bella's short ride on the back of a motorcycle—were shot in **Vancouver, British Columbia (TTTS Book Two)**, around the corner from where exterior Port Angeles movie theatre scenes were filmed for *New Moon*.

Port Angeles—Site 2

🛏 Lodging Options

A Twilicious Port Angeles visit requires less than 3 hours—not counting a second Port Angeles restaurant dining night. Unless you'll be flying into and out of the Port Angeles airport, we recommend lodging in the Forks area. Please see the **Forks Prologue** for Forks area lodging information.

Twilighters who need to lodge in Port Angeles on the night before a return flight from its airport should visit the **TripAdvisor** Port Angeles Bed & Breakfast webpage, where you can also peruse Port Angeles hotel options.
http://www.tripadvisor.com/Hotels-g60921-c2-Port-Angeles-Bed-and-Breakfast.html

🚗 Going to Port Angeles

Port Angeles is perched on Hwy 101—the route between Seattle and Forks—and is only a 1-hour drive northeast of Forks.

Sea-Tac Google Maps SatNav/GPS: 17801 International Boulevard, Seattle, WA 98158

Port Angeles Airport Google Maps SatNav/GPS:
338 West 1st Street, Port Angeles, WA 98362

See the **Airport Options** in Book One's front matter to decide whether to use the Seattle-Tacoma International Airport (Sea-Tac), or Bella's airport (William R. Fairchild International Airport in Port Angeles) as your flight destination when visiting the Olympic Peninsula.

No matter which airport you use, you'll need to **rent a car** to travel to Forks and La Push (discussed in Book One's front matter).

To assist *all* visiting Twilighters, we created a PDF containing a map of the route to Forks from Seattle's airport, and two maps showing Port Angeles Twilight Saga site locations.

[Google Maps segments, married & enhanced, ©2013 Google, above and below]

Tour the Twilight Saga Book One

Tour the Twilight Saga Port Angeles Maps
http://www.TourTheTwilightSaga.com/B1/02PortAngelesMaps.pdf

TTTS Port Angeles Maps Key:

1: Sea-Tac Airport
2: Port Angeles Airport
3: Forks
A: Bella Italia Restaurant
B: Michael's Seafood and Steakhouse
C: The Lincoln Theater
D: Port Book and News
E: Country Aire Natural Food Market (the old Gottschalks department store)
F: The Port Angeles McDonalds
Yellow arrows indicate streets with two-way traffic.
Orange arrows indicate the direction of traffic on one-way streets.

When ready to visit downtown Port Angeles from *any* location, program your SatNav/GPS device with the Bella Italia restaurant address:
118 East 1st Street, Port Angeles, WA 98362.

Drive to the restaurant to orient yourself before looking for a Port Angeles parking place. You may get lucky—as TTTS researchers did—and find a street-side parking spot on Bella Italia's block. If East 1st Street is full, there are plenty of other parking options in the surrounding blocks, including an East 1st Street parking lot on the west side of Michael's.

If you find East 1st Street parking spots full after passing Bella Italia, just keep turning left to check out nearby car parks and street-side parking places on Lincoln, Front, and Laurel streets.

Forks and La Push Prologue

- Tour the Twilight Saga's Forks and La Push Maps
- Forks-Based Twilight Bus Tours
- The Annual Stephenie Meyer Day Celebration
- The Demise of Dazzled By Twilight
- Local Lodging Options

ෆ෮

Tour the Twilight Saga's Forks Walking Tour Map

We developed a walking tour that includes *every* Twilight Saga location found within the town of Forks—all the novel-related places, as well as all the businesses that sell Twilight Saga merchandise. (The Twilight map posted on the Forks Chamber of Commerce website is wonderful, but it doesn't include all the Twilight Saga merchandise businesses.)

Our Forks Walking Tour Map is Posted Online

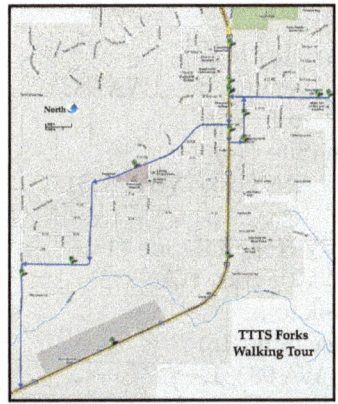

[Google Maps segments, married & enhanced, ©2013 Google]
http://www.TourTheTwilightSaga.com/B1/MapsForksLaPush.pdf

Tour the Twilight Saga Book One

The Forks Walking Tour Map Key

A: Forks Chamber of Commerce & Visitor Center (Site #4)
Our full Forks Twilight Saga walking tour begins and ends at the Forks Chamber of Commerce and Visitor Center (COC). After all, the COC is a must-visit site, and it has a large parking lot.
1411 South Forks Avenue, Forks, WA 98331
An 11 minute walk to …

B: Forks Outfitters & the Thriftway (Site #5)
950 South Forks Avenue Forks, WA 98331
A 9 minute walk to …

C: Forks Coffee Shop (Site #6)
314 South Forks Avenue, Forks, WA 98331
A 2 minute walk to …

D: Forks High School Sign (Site #7)
261 Spartan Avenue, Forks, WA 98331
A 1 minute walk to …

E: Leppell's Flowers & Gifts (Site #8)
130 Spartan Ave, Forks, WA 98331
An 8 minute walk to …

F: Forks Police Department (Site #9)
500 E Division St, Forks, WA 98331
A 1 minute walk to …

G: The Miller Tree Inn—aka the **Cullen House** in Forks (Site #10)
654 E Division St, Forks, WA 98331
A 7 minute walk to …

H: Native to Twilight Store (Site #11)
10 North Forks Avenue, Forks, WA 98331
A 1 minute walk to …

I: TwiFoot Tours Office (Site #12)
51 North Forks Avenue, Forks, WA 98331
A 1 minute walk to …

J: JT's Sweet Stuffs (Site #13)
80 North Forks Avenue, Forks, WA 98331
A 2 minute walk to …

K: Sully's Drive-In (Site #14)
220 North Forks Ave, Forks, WA 98331
A 6 minute walk to …

L: Forks Community Hospital (Site #15)
530 Bogachiel Way, Forks, WA 98331
A 10 minute walk to …

M: The Swan House (Site #16)
775 K St, Forks, WA 98331
A 4 minute walk to …

Forks & La Push Prologue

N: The Discarded Motorcycles Location (Site #17)
Russell Road, Forks, WA 98331
A 16 minute walk back to the Forks Chamber of Commerce.

Timing Your Forks Twilight Saga Walking Tour

To walk between all 14 Forks Twilight Saga sites requires at least 90 minutes. Because the amount of time you may wish to spend at each site varies, we used the following suggested visit times to estimate a *minimum* total tour time to schedule:

- 1 hour at the Forks Chamber of Commerce & Visitor Center
- 45 minutes to eat at *one* of the Twilight-Saga-related Forks restaurants
 (You can dine at either of the other two on another day.)
- 20 minutes to snap exterior pix at each of the places you cannot enter
- 45 minutes to shop at each store that sells Twilight Saga merchandise

The Result: 8 Hours

Yes, that's a long day—but it's doable. The greatest between-site distance is only a 16 minute walk, and all the other walks are quite short. It's the shopping time that makes this itinerary so long.

Twilighters who schedule **three days** to visit Forks and La Push can split the full Twilight Saga Forks tour into two parts: a Forks sites drive day and a Forks sites walk day. These two-part tour maps are included in our Forks Walking Tour PDF.

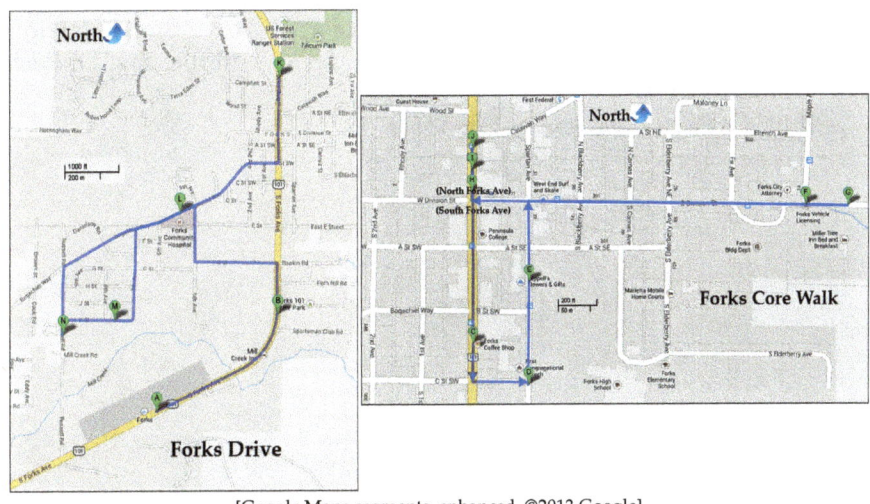

[Google Maps segments, enhanced, ©2013 Google]

Tour the Twilight Saga Book One

Forks Drive Day: Visit the **COC**, then drive to the four Twilight Saga Sites seen on the large loop of our full Walking Tour Map, ending with a meal at **Sully's** (map point K, Site #14).

Forks Drive Itinerary: 3 hours, 45 minutes—including an hour at the COC.

Forks Core Walk Day: Park at **Forks Coffee Shop** (map point C, Site #6). After your meal (approximately 45 minutes), walk to the seven other core Forks Twilight Saga sites. Enjoy a snack at **JT's Sweet Shop** (map point J, Site #13) before heading back to your car.

Forks Core Walk Tour Itinerary: 3 hours, 15 minutes.

The total visit time required for any of our Forks Twilight Saga tour itineraries is much shorter if you'll be riding on one of the **Twilight Tour Busses** (see below). Bus-riding Twilighters do not need to drive or walk to Forks Community Hospital, the Swan House, Russell Road, Forks High School, Forks Police Department, or the Cullen House in Forks.

After reading each Forks site chapter, it's easy to determine which places you'll be happy to visit solely via tour bus, which ones you'll want to trek to privately, and when to do so.

Tour the Twilight Saga La Push Drive Map

Our La Push Driving Tour itinerary includes *every* Twilight Saga location between the city of Forks and First Beach in La Push—all novel-related places, and all businesses that sell Twilight Saga merchandise. We've also included two tide pool beaches for intrepid Twilighters with extra time.

Our map begins at the Forks Chamber of Commerce Visitor Center for reference purposes only. You can start the La Push Drive from *any* Forks location by programming your SatNav/GPS device with the first La Push Drive site's address:

🚗 100 La Push Road, Forks, WA 98331

Forks & La Push Prologue

Our La Push Drive Map is Posted Online
(It's in the same PDF that contains our Forks Tour Maps.)

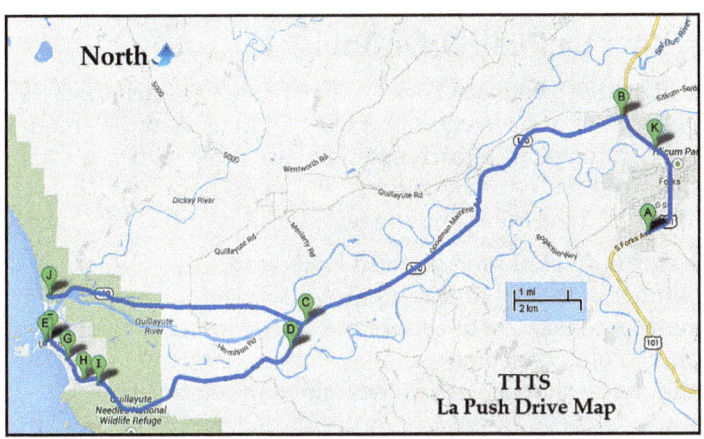

[Google Maps segment, enhanced, ©2013 Google]
http://www.TourTheTwilightSaga.com/B1/MapsForksLaPush.pdf

La Push Drive Map Key

A: Forks Chamber of Commerce & Visitor Center (Site #4)
1411 South Forks Avenue, Forks, WA 98331
B: Old Mill Trading Post (Site #18)
100 La Push Road, Forks, WA 98331
C: The Treaty Line Sign (Site #19)
7765 La Push Rd, Forks, WA 98331
D: Jacob Black's House & The Wolf Den (Site #20)
8320 La Push Road, Forks, WA 98331
E: La Push First Beach (Site #21)
Parking Lot Coordinates: 47.908245,-124.63981
F: Quileute Reservation & Old (Lower) Village (Site #22)
30 River St, La Push WA 98350
G: Lonesome Creek Store and **Oceanside Resort Gift Shop** (info within Site #22)
490 Ocean Dr, La Push, WA 98350
H: La Push Second Beach Parking Lot (a tide pool beach option, info within Site #21)
Coordinates: 47.898147,-124.623502
I: The Akalat Center (info within Site #22)
Coordinates: 47.89724,-124.617194
J: Rialto Beach Parking Lot (a tide pool beach option, info within Site #21)
Coordinates: 47.920627,-124.637643

K: **The Northern Forks Welcome Sign** (Site #3)
47.959238,-124.391972

Timing Your La Push Drive Tour

The roundtrip drive between Forks and La Push—*not* including either of the tide pool beach options—requires at least an hour, and the amount of time you may wish to spend at each site will vary. Our *minimum* total La Push Drive itinerary time estimate is based on a one hour drive between Forks and La Push, and the following suggested visit times:

- At least 1 hour exploring La Push First Beach
- 45 minutes at the old (lower) Quileute Village
- 20 minutes to take pix at each of the places you cannot enter, and the northern Forks Welcome sign
- 45 minutes to shop at each of the four shops on the map.

The Result: 7 hours

Again, this is the minimum amount of tour time to plan for. You may want to stay longer at some of these sites—especially First Beach. If visiting the Quileute Community Center on a Wednesday, you can attend a **Healing Circle/Drum Group** from 5:30 to 9:30pm. In addition, you may decide to trek to the tide pools at **Second Beach** *or* **Rialto Beach**, either of which will extend your La Push Drive Tour by another 1 hour and 45 minutes—possibly 2 hours.

Three of the La Push Drive sites (the Treaty Sign, Jacob Black's house, and the Wolf Den) are sufficiently visited by the Twifoot Tour bus and won't require a private stop by bus-riding Twilighters. Skipping those places will save you an hour when planning your private—*perfect*—La Push tour. Additionally, the Old Mill Trading Post (Site #18) is close enough to Forks that it can easily be visited on another day of your holiday, saving another 45 minutes.

Again, after reading each Forks and La Push site chapter, it's easy to determine which places you'll be happy to visit solely via tour bus, which ones you'll want to trek to privately, and when to do so.

Forks & La Push Prologue

[©2013 CD Miller]

Forks-Based Twilight Bus Tours

As of September, 2013, there are two of them:

- **Team Forks Twilight Tours**, run by Charlene Leppell, owner of **Leppell's Flowers & Gifts** (Site #8).
  http://www.teamforks.com/
- **TwiFoot Twilight Tours** (Site #12), run by Nino and Rosemary Colandrea, two incredibly talented and personable Forks residents. In addition to their Twilight Tours, they also offer fabulous **Big Foot** tours of the Olympic Peninsula's **Hoh Rainforest**. If you want to go *Squatchin'* in addition to touring the Twilight Saga, book both TwiFoot Tours while you're in Forks!
  http://www.twifoottours.com/

Twilight Saga Sites Visited by *Both* Forks Twilight Tour Companies:

- Forks Chamber of Commerce (Site #4)
  This is only a brief stop—mostly for Bella Truck pic-taking. Visit the COC on your own to enjoy all that it has to offer.
- Forks High School Sign (Site #7)
- Forks Police Department (Site #9)
- The Miller Tree Inn Cullen House (Site #10)
- Forks Community Hospital (Site #15)
- The Swan House (Site #16)
- The Russell Road Discarded Motorcycles Location (Site #17)

Tour the Twilight Saga Book One

Twilight Saga Sites Best Visited via the Twifoot Tour Bus:
- The Quileute Reservation Treaty Line Sign (Site #19)
- Jacob Black's House & The Wolf Den (Site #20)
- La Push First Beach (Site #21)
  This is only a brief stop. To fully enjoy First Beach, trek there on your own, as well.
- The Northern Welcome to Forks Sign (Site #3)

Twilight Saga Sites *not* Visited by *either* Tour Company:
- Forks Outfitters (Site #5)
- Forks Coffee Shop (Site #6)
- Native to Twilight Store (Site #11)
- JT's Sweet Stuffs (Site #13)
- Sully's Drive-In (Site #14)
- Old Mill Trading Post (Site #18)
- The Quileute Old Village (Site #22)
- Jacob's Tribal School (info in Site #22)
- Lonesome Creek Store and Quileute Oceanside Resort Gift Shop (info in Site #22)
- The tide pools at Second Beach or Rialto Beach (info in Site #21)
- Westlands Homestead (Site #23) — the real-world Cullen House

Tour the Twilight Saga Recommendation

Book a TwiFoot Twilight Tour of Forks *and* La Push on one of your days in the area. If Nino and Rosemary are booked, sign up for a Leppell's Team Forks tour, and visit all the La Push sites on your own. Then, privately visit all the places where Forks Twilight tour busses don't stop on another day.

Forks & La Push Prologue

[©2013 Tara Miller]

The Annual Stephenie Meyer Day Celebration in Forks

Soon after the town began enjoying the tourism surge spawned by the 2005 publication of her first novel, Stephenie Meyer traveled to Forks to do a book-signing event and was honored by Mayor Nedra Reed, who declared **July 20th, 2006**, an honorary **Stephenie Meyer Day**. Only 250 fans happened to be on hand that day, but the number of Forks-visiting Twilighters significantly increased in 2006, and *exploded* in 2007. Thus, the Forks COC created an annual Stephenie Meyer Day (SMD). As **Marcia Bingham**, COC Customer Service Director, explained in the *Twilight in Forks* documentary:

> "We wanted it to be [Stephenie's] birthday, but her birthday is Christmas Eve. [Winter is *not* the best time to visit Washington's Olympic Peninsula.] So we picked Bella's birthday, **September 13th**. And we made that our big party day."

The first September SMD celebration was a one-day event in 2007. As more Twilighters learned about it, the celebration increased to two days in 2008. Since 2009, the September SMD celebration has become an annual **three-day event**. The SMD weekend has grown to become so jam-packed full of special events, those who want to enjoy every Twilicious tidbit need to schedule at least *five days* when visiting Forks and La Push during SMD.

[Facebook.com/StephenieMeyerDays2013 Profile Pic]

Tips for Planning a Stephenie Meyer Day Celebration Visit

Step One: If you can travel to Forks in September, the first planning resources to explore are the website and Facebook pages run by the *original* **Stephenie Meyer Days Organization**:
http://www.stepheniemeyerdays2013.com/
https://www.facebook.com/StephenieMeyerDays2013

> "The purpose of this event is to recognize the talents of Stephenie Meyer, provide a fun filled weekend, and showcase our local businesses & community!"

The original SMD organization's Internet-address changes each year. Replace 2013 with 2014, and so on.

This group is special because they are a Forks Community Organization that fosters SMD participation of *all* local businesses in town. And, the majority of their events are **free**.

A Few Highlights from the SMD 2013 Schedule:

- Forks Music Festival at the Round House — Free.
- Blood Drive at the Forks Community Hospital — Free (They don't charge to take your blood!)
- Bella's Baby Shower — A donation for the Forks children's charity, **Bundles for Babes**, was required. Twilighters were encouraged to pick up some baby supplies at the Thriftway, and bring them in. Cash donations were also accepted.
- Quileute Storytelling on First Beach — Free

http://www.stepheniemeyerdays2013.com/stephenie-meyer-days-2013-schedule-of-events.html

Forks & La Push Prologue

In 2013, the original SMD group's Special Guests were **Hannah and Hilly Hindi**, of **The Hillywood Show**.
http://www.thehillywoodshow.com/

> "The Hillywood Show® is the brainchild of [YouTube] Internet celebrities, comedy sister duo Hilly & Hannah Hindi. Each parody features satire sketches, character impersonations, song & dance parodies of the big box office films such as Twilight & Harry Potter along with popular TV shows … Their incredible costumes & makeup would impress even the most seasoned Saturday Night Live cast member!"

If you've never seen the Hillywood Twilight Parody videos, you *must* go to their YouTube channel and watch them.
http://www.youtube.com/user/JckSparrow

[Profile photo from the **SMD2** Facebook page (enhanced), ©2013]

Step Two: Check out the *secondary* **Stephenie Meyer Day** (SMD2) organization's website and Facebook page.
http://www.stepheniemeyerday.com/
https://www.facebook.com/StephenieMeyerDay

> **Please Note:** Because this group is not associated with Forks' local merchants and the Forks Chamber of Commerce, there is no guarantee that it will exist after 2013.

The SMD2 group is run by Staci Chastain—the owner of **Alice's Closet**, a Twilight Saga replica costume boutique once located in Forks that closed in June of 2013. The SMD2 group includes a troop of Twihards known as the **Olympic Coven**. The Olympic Coven cast changes from year to year, and performers hale from places all over the US, such as New York, Florida, and Connecticut. The Olympic Coven has members who look somewhat similar to Twilight Saga actors, and all don amazingly accurate replica costumes when performing as Twilight Saga look-alikes during SMD2 events.

[©2013 Tara Miller]

On Thursday, September 12th, the 2013 Olympic Coven made a free appearance at the **Mill Creek Bar** in Forks. It was pretty exciting for those of us who'd never been to a Cosplay event before.
http://en.wikipedia.org/wiki/Cosplay

[©2013 CD Miller]

In 2013, SMD2 teamed up with **Forever in Forks** (FIF), an organization based in Phoenix, Arizona.
http://www.foreverinforks.com/

> "Forever in Forks is an organization dedicated to bringing Twilight fans together once a year in a different Twilight-related city to celebrate the books and films we love, while raising money for a charitable cause."

Forks & La Push Prologue

All of the 2013 SMD2/FIF Events Were Ticketed

If you didn't purchase tickets in advance (online), there was no guarantee that they'd be available during your September visit. Unfortunately, only the Saturday night **Forever Party** ticket was available *separately*. All other 2013 SMD2/FIF events could only be attended if you pre-purchased a **Full Package** ticket.

- The 2013 SMD2/FIF Full Package ticket: $200
- The 2013 SMD2/FIF Forever Party ticket: $125

According to the SMD2 and FIF websites, all proceeds from their 2013 ticket sales—after expenses were paid—were donated to the (non-Forks) charity, **Stand Up 2 Cancer.**
http://www.standup2cancer.org/custom/?c=team&a=index&id=7967#

> **Please Note:** Every charity has a responsibility to contribute what they commit to donate on behalf of the people who purchase tickets. In order to make sure your charity donation goes to the people it was intended for, please ask for an accounting of the donation given after the event takes place. If enough people ask on Facebook and other public venues, charities will have to make a public accounting of their donations.

The Dazzled By Twilight Question

Twilighters who've seen the Forks documentaries may be wondering, "What ever happened to that **Dazzled by Twilight** store?"

The short answer: The last of their businesses closed in January of 2012, and the Dazzled by Twilight dynasty longer exists.

For Twihards interested in the long answer, we created a PDF containing the full story of Dazzled by Twilight's rapid rise to fame, and equally rapid demise—an account that exposes the unfortunate behavior associated with Dazzled by Twilight.
http://www.TourTheTwilightSaga.com/B1/DBTstory.pdf

Tour the Twilight Saga Book One

[*Twilight In Forks* screenshot segments (enhanced)]

🛏 Forks and La Push Lodging Options

To decide where to stay during a visit to Forks/La Push, begin by reading the chapters about Twilight Saga sites that happen to be lodging establishments.

- Site #10: **Miller Tree Inn Bed & Breakfast**—aka the Cullen House in Forks
- Site #19: **Three Rivers Resort**, home of the Treaty Line Sign
- Site #20: **Jacob Black's House & The Wolf Den**
- Site #23: **Beaver Creek Cabins** at **Westlands Homestead**—the real-world Cullen House

To explore all available lodgings in the area—including those on the Quileute Reservation—go to the Forks Chamber of Commerce lodging directory. It's extensive.
http://forkswa.com/business-directory/lodging/

You can read reviews of these lodgings on **TripAdvisor.com**. For example, if you search "Forks Motel, Forks, Washington" on TripAdvisor you'll find:
http://www.tripadvisor.com/Hotel_Review-g58476-d100478-Reviews-Forks_Motel-Forks_Washington.html

Forks & La Push Prologue

[©2013 CD Miller]

Tour the Twilight Saga suggests lodging at least one night at the **Miller Tree Inn** (Site #10)—the Cullen House in Forks—so that you can enjoy all of Bill and Susan Brager's Twilight Saga attractions.

[©2013 CD Miller]

As for the other nights of your Forks/La Push visit, if your party consists of two or more people, our favorite Forks area lodging is **Beaver Creek Cabins**, found at the original Cullen House—**Westlands Homestead** (Site #23). In fact, we loved this place so much, it was the sole subject of the very first vid we posted on the TTTS YouTube Channel:
http://www.youtube.com/watch?v=6Ja4cNp5yL8

Bottom Line: no matter where you stay in the Forks/La Push area, or how long you're able to stay, you are going to have a Twilicious time visiting the Twilight Saga novel locations in the Olympic Peninsula of Washington State.

Tour the Twilight Saga Book One

3

City of Forks Welcomes You Sign

Google Maps & SatNav/GPS Coordinates
Northern Sign: 47.959238,-124.391972
Southern Sign: 1411 South Forks Avenue, Forks, WA 98331

Visit Time: 10 to 15 minutes, per sign.

☙❧

Yes, there are two **Forks Welcomes You** signs—one at the north end of town and one at the south end. Both are on Highway 101.

[*Destination Forks* screenshot segment (enhanced)]

Tour the Twilight Saga Book One

When arriving in Forks from Port Angeles/Seattle, you'll be greeted by the northern sign. This is the most photogenic of the two signs, because of the shrubberies and trees behind it. If it's clear and sunny when you arrive, snap your welcome sign pix right away—it might be raining during other photo ops here.

[2008 Street view image segment (enhanced), ©2013 Google]

If you use the northern sign's coordinates as your first destination when driving to Forks from the north, look to the right just before reaching it. There is a large lay-by in front of a gated driveway where you can briefly park while sign-pic snapping. The Twifoot Tour bus parks here to allow photo op time. You'll also pass this sign when returning to Forks after visiting **La Push First Beach** and the **Quileute Reservation** (Sites 21 & 22).

[©2013 Tara Miller]

Twilighters arriving from the south (Saint Helens/Portland, Oregon) will see the southern welcome sign first. It's at the **Forks Chamber of Commerce Visitor Center** (Site #4), in front of the **Forks Timber Museum**.

City of Forks Welcomes You Sign—Site 3

[*Twilight* screenshot segment (enhanced)]

Prior to the *Twilight* movie's release, the southern sign was located about a block farther south, just off the side of the road, in a setting similar to what was seen on screen. When Twilighters began flocking to Forks, there was no place to safely pull over and snap sign pix. To prevent accidents and injuries, the sign was moved to the Chamber of Commerce, where there is plenty of parking.

Tour the Twilight Saga Book One

4

The Forks Chamber of Commerce Visitor Center

Forks Chamber of Commerce website: http://forkswa.com/
Forks Community website: http://www.forkswashington.org/

Google Maps & SatNav/GPS: 1411 South Forks Avenue, Forks, WA 98331

Hours of Operation: Tourist Season, 10am to 5pm; Off-Season, 10am to 4pm; Sundays all year-round, 10am to 4pm.

Visit Time: Plan on spending at least an hour here to explore the visitor center and a few of its many attractions. Scheduling two hours here would be even better.

[©2013 CD Miller]

Tour the Twilight Saga Book One

The **Forks Chamber of Commerce Visitor Center** (COC) is the perfect starting point for a Twilight Saga tour of Forks. In addition to being the home of the southern **Forks Welcomes You** sign (Site #3), the COC offers a wealth of Twilicious information, displays and souvenirs, as well as several other extremely interesting non-*Twilight* attractions.

[©2013 Tara Miller]

Stephenie Meyer's Twilight Saga novels have been a huge boon to the Forks tourist economy. Following *Twilight*'s October 2005 publication, a record 6,000 people signed the COC guest book in 2006. Visitor signatures jumped to 10,000 in 2007, and skyrocketed to 18,736 in 2008. After the *Twilight* movie's November 2008 release, more than *55,600* people signed the book in 2009! As each new Twilight Saga movie hit the screen, visitor numbers continued to multiply.

According to **Marcia Bingham**, COC Director of Customer Service:

> "[Stephenie Meyer] placed the book in Forks because she Googled 'wet dark and rainy' … We won the lottery big-time on that because [the Twilight Saga has] been so good for our economy and our people. … The biggest joy to me now, is when people come to Forks and it's rainy and they're *thrilled*. If it's sunny, they complain. This is *not* something we've heard in the past. So it's great!"

Thus, it comes as no surprise that COC staff members are thrilled to do everything possible to ensure that Twilighters thoroughly enjoy their visit to Forks.

The Forks Chamber of Commerce Visitor Center—Site 4

[©2013 Tara Miller]

As soon as you pull into the parking lot, you'll see Bella's truck!

Early in the Twilight Saga tourist boom, the COC managed to obtain a 1952 Chevrolet truck exactly like the novel's description of the '51 Chevy truck that Charlie bought for Bella as a welcome home present.

> "It was a faded red color, with big, rounded fenders and a bulbous cab. To my intense surprise, I loved it."

[©2013 Tara Miller]

During the 2010 Stephenie Meyer Day celebration in Forks (see our Forks Prologue for SMD information), the **Elwha River Casino** of Port Angeles held a drawing for a 1963 Chevrolet truck almost exactly like the one seen on screen. Strangely enough, the winner elected to accept a $2,000 cash prize rather than take the truck—yet another "big lottery win" for the Forks COC.

Tour the Twilight Saga Book One

Why? Because, after paying out the cash prize, the Elwha River casino graciously donated the truck to them. Thus, the Forks Visitor Center has both the novel and movie versions of Bella's truck for Twilighters to take pix of.
http://www.elwharivercasino.com/

[*Twilight* screenshot segment (enhanced)]

Each of the Bella truck cabs are kept locked to prevent damage due to thousands of Twilighter tushes sliding in and out. Carefully climbing into the box of the movie pickup, however, *is* permitted. If your party includes an Emmett stand-in, snap pix of him in the back of Bella's truck.

After taking Bella truck pix, go inside the Forks Chamber of Commerce Visitor Center. Sign the Guest Book and pick up their free **Twilight Packet**, which includes:

- A copy of the **Forks Twilight Map** (also offered online). It's a great souvenir, even though it includes only a few of the sites found on Tour the Twilight Saga maps.
- **Driving Directions** for a self-guided tour of the COC-identified Twilight sights.
- **Trivia Tests** that challenge your knowledge of all four Twilight Saga novels.
- Information about five fabulous non-*Twilight* **Day Trips** you can enjoy while visiting Forks and Washington's Olympic Peninsula.

The Forks Chamber of Commerce Visitor Center—Site 4

[©2013 CD Miller]

Be sure to push a pin into their World wall map, or USA wall map, to represent your place of origin—*if* you can find a spot not already full of pins!

[*Twilight In Forks* screenshot segment (enhanced)]

Page through notebooks full of mail that has been sent from all over the world to Bella, Edward, and other Cullen family members, in *care-of* the Forks Chamber of Commerce.

[©2013 CD Miller]

Tour the Twilight Saga Book One

Shop! Several Forks and Twilight Saga T-shirts unique to the COC are available, along with loads of inexpensive souvenirs.

[©2013 CD Miller]

Both Twilight Tour bus companies make brief stops for Bella truck pic-taking and a quick visit inside the COC. We highly recommend making a private stop as well, to fully enjoy *all* that the Forks visitor center offers.

[©2013 CD Miller]

Next door to the Forks COC is the Forks Timber Museum.

> "The museum displays exhibits depicting local history dating back to the 1870s. Constructed in 1990 by the Forks High School carpentry class, the 3,200 square foot building provides a fascinating look back into the local history of the timber industry."

http://www.forks-web.com/fg/timbermuseum.htm

The Forks Chamber of Commerce Visitor Center—Site 4

[©2013 Tara Miller]

Beside the Timber Museum is a small **Soroptimist International** garden. Behind that (where the lady in pink is seen above), you'll find the entrance to a short forest trail that offers a 15 minute glimpse of what the **Hoh Rain Forrest** looks like.

[©2013 Tara Miller]

The gentle, fern-lined path leads from the Soroptimist garden to the COC parking lot. After passing beneath trees dripping with moss, you'll soon reach a gigantic old tree stump that is hollow—go inside! The photo below was taken inside, looking up to the forest canopy high above.

[©2013 CD Miller]

Hopefully, this glimpse will inspire you to *go to* the Hoh Rain Forest. Although 3 to 4 hours are required to fully appreciate its wonders, Twilighters in a rush can enjoy a quickie trip there—accomplished in little more than an hour. Read our **Hoh Rain Forest Trip Tips** to learn more.
http://www.TourTheTwilightSaga.com/B1/HOHtips.pdf

Lastly, you never know who you might run into when visiting the Forks Chamber of Commerce and Visitor Center.

[©2013 Tara Miller]

During the September 2013 Stephenie Meyer Day celebration, Stephenie Meyer surprised everyone—including the Forks Police Department and Chamber of Commerce—by showing up on the eve of Bella's birthday!

The Forks Chamber of Commerce Visitor Center—Site 4

She spent Friday morning signing autographs and posing for fan photos at the COC, visited **Sully's Drive In** (Site #14) for lunch, and finished the afternoon at **La Push First Beach** (Site #21). Later that evening she was sighted at the **Bella Italia** restaurant in Port Angeles (Site #2).

[©2013 CD Miller]

Because we were on the TwiFoot tour at the time, Tara and Chas were taken to the head of the Stephenie Meyer line. You can watch footage of this fabulous treat on Tour the Twilight Saga's YouTube Channel.
http://www.youtube.com/watch?v=XUVc7KOqebg

[©2013 CD Miller]

2013 was Stephenie's first trip to Forks since her *Twilight* book-signing event in July of 2006. In reality, it's unlikely that you'll run into her. But, visiting Forks during the annual Stephenie Meyer Day celebration certainly will increase your chances!

Tour the Twilight Saga Book One

5

Forks Outfitters and the Thriftway

Aka Newton's Olympic Outfitters and Fork's Thriftway
http://www.forksoutfitters.com/
http://www.forksthriftway.com/
https://www.facebook.com/shopforksoutfitters

Google Maps & SatNav/GPS: 950 South Forks Avenue Forks, WA 98331

Hours of Operation: Open daily from 8am to 9pm, closed on Thanksgiving and Christmas Day

Visit Time: At least a 45 minute Twilight Saga shopping sprint.

[©2013 Tara Miller]

Tour the Twilight Saga Book One

Forks Outfitters is the outdoor apparel and sporting goods store where Bella worked part-time for Mike's parents, which is why it's called **Newton's Olympic Outfitters** in the novels. In real life, it's attached to the local **Thriftway** grocery store, also mentioned in *Twilight*.

> "I had my shopping list and the cash from the jar in the cupboard labeled FOOD MONEY, and I was on my way to the Thriftway."

[©2013 CD Miller, above and below]

The Thriftway store has a small Twilight Zone at the front of the store, and also sells a variety of inexpensive native art souvenirs amid the grocery isles.

Forks Outfitters and the Thriftway—Site 5

[©2013 CD Miller]

Forks Outfitters has a terrific selection of Twilight and Forks t-shirts. If the High School is closed during your visit (Site #7), get your Spartan gear here.

[*Twilight In Forks* screenshot segment (enhanced)]

And, yes, Forks Outfitters still sells Bella Swan employee ID tags!

Deserving an Honorable Mention: the Thriftway Espresso Café

This is one of only *two* places in Forks where you can purchase a full-bodied cup of coffee, with or without barista fru-fru. (The **Mocha Motion Espresso** drive-through is the other place, located across the street from **Forks Coffee Shop**, Site #6.) Thriftway Espresso's teas, smoothies, and Italian sodas are also deliciously full-flavored.

[©2013 CD Miller]

They also feature a special Twilight beverage menu

- **Twilight Tea:** A Chai Latte made with (non-alcoholic) Irish Cream.
- **New Moon Mocha:** A smooth blend of Hershey's and white chocolate, with a bite of raspberry.
- **Eclipse Energizer:** A Red Bull with a shot of Bev Rev [caffeine syrup], black cherry and vanilla flavoring—get ready to gain Vampire speed!
- **Breaking Dawn Brevé:** A latte made with espresso and steamed half-and-half (instead of milk), caramel sauce, and French vanilla syrup.

6

Forks Coffee Shop

http://www.forkscoffeeshop.com/
http://forkswa.com/listing/forks-coffee-shop/

Google Maps & SatNav/GPS: 241 South Forks Avenue, Forks, WA 98331

Hours of Operation: Open daily from 5:30am to 8pm.

Visit Time: Plan at least 45 minutes to eat here and snap pix.

Please Note: See important Forks parking info at the end of this chapter.

[©2013 CD Miller]

Forks Coffee Shop is where Chief Charlie Swan frequently ate dinner before Bella moved home and began cooking for him.

[*Twilight* screenshot (enhanced)]

If the Twilight Saga movies had been filmed in Forks, Charlie and Bella diner scenes—as well as Stephenie Meyer's *Twilight* cameo—would have been shot here. Instead, these scenes were filmed in Oregon, at the **Damascus Carver Café** (TTTS Book Three).

[©2013 CD Miller]

The Forks Coffee Shop is a full service restaurant, featuring delicious daily specials, homemade soups and desserts. Breakfast items are served all day long. Their lunch menu includes a Garden Burger (Bella's veggie burger), and Bella's favorite Berry Cobbler is always available.

Twilighters *must* eat here at least once during a Twilight Saga visit. Also, be sure to keep Forks Coffee Shop in mind when you need something to go!

Forks Coffee Shop—Site 6

ଓଃଓ

Forks Parking and Coffee Tips

Forks has short-term, metered street parking, and two pay-parking lots.

[©2013 CD Miller]

The Forks Coffee Shop parking lot should only be used while eating in the diner. The best place to park when you need to leave your car for a few hours—such as when enjoying a Twilight tour or walking to Twi-themed stores—is the gravel lot across the street from Forks Coffee Shop.

[©2013 CD Miller]

Also located in this lot is the **Mocha Motion Espresso** drive-through. This is one of only *two* places in Forks where you can purchase a full-bodied cup of coffee. (The **Thriftway Espresso Bar** is the other place, and is mentioned in **Forks Outfitters**, Site #5.) Mocha Motion also offers delicious teas, cocoa, and fruit smoothies.

To watch some hilarious Mocha Motion footage shot by Chas when she and Tara visited in September of 2013, go to the link below.
http://www.youtube.com/watch?v=67N7AiBQGpo

7

Forks High School

http://quillayute.hs.schooldesk.net/
http://www.forks.wednet.edu/
http://en.wikipedia.org/wiki/Forks_High_School

Google Maps & SatNav/GPS: 261 South Spartan Avenue, Forks, WA 98331

Administration Office Hours: Monday through Friday, 7:30am to 4:30pm. Closed in July and most of August.

Visit Time: 20 minutes is sufficient for snapping pix in front of the Forks High School sign. Add another 30 minutes to visit the Admin Office and purchase authentic Spartan gear and souvenirs. During Stephenie Meyer Days in September, additional school access may be available.

[*Twilight in Forks* screenshot segment (enhanced)]

Tour the Twilight Saga Book One

When constructed in 1925, **Forks High School** was called **Quillayute High School**—thus the sign above the old school's main entrance that many Twilighters have found confusing. Even today, Forks High School remains part of the *Quillayute* Valley Schools District (QVSD), which includes all schools in Forks and on the *Quileute* Reservation.

> **Please Note:** "Quileute" is the spelling preferred by the Quileute people. "Quillayute," an Americanized spelling, is also acceptable.
> http://en.wikipedia.org/wiki/Quileute_people

[©2009 Rachel Raymond (enhanced)]   [©2010 Discover Forks Facebook]

Sadly, the old Forks High School—the one Bella attended—was closed after being condemned in 2008, and completely demolished in 2010. Constructed on the same site, a brand new Forks High School opened in January of 2012.

[©2013 Tara Miller]

Historically important portions of the original high school were preserved and incorporated when constructing the new one. The old terracotta and brick front entrance elements—including the Quillayute High School capstone sign with its beautiful scrollwork—were restored and installed *inside* the main entrance, to protect them from future weather damage.

Forks High School—Site 7

Forks High School Spartans Sign Prior to Demolition
[Internet-posted photo segment (enhanced), ©unknown]

Happy Twilighters! The QVSD also considered the old Forks High School Spartans sign worthy of preservation—primarily due to its Twilight Saga importance to Forks tourism.

[*Twilight* screenshot segment (enhanced)]

After all, this is the sign that was reproduced by filmmakers and installed outside **Kalama High School** in Kalama, Washington (TTTS Book Three), where they shot exterior Forks High School scenes.

Forks High School Spartans Sign History

The original Forks High School Spartans sign was crafted by prisoners who worked in the wood shop at the nearby **Olympic Corrections Center**. The sign was finished and installed in 1996, when the old high school was 71 years old.
http://www.doc.wa.gov/facilities/prison/occ/

Just prior to demolition of the old high school in 2010, the original Forks Spartans sign was carefully removed, cleaned, and stored until it could be installed in front of the new school's main entrance before its grand opening in January of 2012.

Soon after that, however, the QVSD again contacted the Olympic Corrections wood shop, requesting the creation of an exact replica of the 1996 Forks High School Spartans sign — same size, same lettering, same Spartan Warrior image and paint scheme.

Why? Because the original school sign had suffered serious deterioration over the years due to the extremes of Forks' weather, and the QVSD wanted a new sign to post in front of the new school. But, they also wanted to ensure the continued interest of Twilighters wishing to pose in front of Bella's high school sign.

[©2013 Tara Miller]

Thus, the sign now found in front of Forks High School is an exact replica of the 1996 sign.

Rumor has it that the original, sadly deteriorated, 1996 sign was sold at auction — perhaps even on EBay! While some Twihards may consider this a sacrilegious act, all funds obtained from the sign's sale were donated to Forks High School, and thus benefited the Forks student body.

Bottom Line: While it might not be the original sign reproduced by filmmakers, Twilighters will always have an exact replica of the 1996 Forks High School Home of the Spartans sign to visit and pose with.

Visiting Forks High School

The halls and classrooms of Forks High School are *not* open to the public.

Real-world safety and security of Forks school children outweighs any Twihard's desire to wander willy-nilly within Bella Swan's high school.

Forks High School—Site 7

Twilighters are welcome to snap pix in front of the Forks High School Spartan sign on any day, at any time. But, please abide by the **Twilight Treaty**. Avoid including students in your photos, and do not enter the school building—*apart from* stepping inside the **main entrance**, and turning left to enter the **Forks High School Administration Office**.

[©2013 CD Miller]

When it is open, the folks who staff Forks High School Admin Office are happy to greet you, and even happier to sell you **authentic Forks High School Spartans apparel and souvenirs.** Yes, the Spartan gear selection offered at the Admin Office may be rather sparse. (The items seen above are all that were available when Chas and Tara visited in September of 2013.) But, proceeds from Spartan t-shirts and paraphernalia purchased at Forks High School financially benefit the Forks High School student body.

[©2013 CD Miller]

Spartan gear knockoffs are available elsewhere in Forks.

Spartan gear available at Forks Outfitters (Site #5) is seen above, left. Spartan gear available at Leppell's Flowers & Gifts (Site #8) is seen above, right.

Because the sale of Spartan clothing and souvenirs purchased elsewhere doesn't benefit the Forks High School student body, however, we suggest that: if you don't find what you'd like to buy when visiting Forks High School's Admin Office—or if it isn't open during your visit—shop the Forks High School online Spartan Gear store after you get home.
http://www.spiritshop.com/school/washington/forks/forks_high_school-11957.aspx?kw=fb&utm_source=fb

8

Leppell's Flowers and Gifts Team Forks Twilight Tour

https://www.facebook.com/Leppellstwilightcentral
http://forkswa.com/listing/twilight-central-leppells-flowers-and-gifts/

Google Maps & SatNav/GPS: 130 South Spartan Avenue, Forks, WA 98331

Hours of Operation: Monday-Saturday, 10am to 5:30pm; Sundays, 11am to 3pm.

Visit Time: Plan at least 45 minutes to shop, and shop, and shop!

[©2013 CD Miller]

Tour the Twilight Saga Book One

Leppell's Flowers and Gifts—aka **Twilight Central**—is run by owner Charlene Cross-Leppell.

> "We are a small town florist with a flare for Twilight! We offer not only a smile and hello when you walk in the door, but a wide variety of Twilight merchandise too! We have many things designed and crafted by local artists, as well as exclusive Twilight inspired themed clothing designs that are made on premises."

[©2013 CD Miller, above left and below] [©2013 Tara Miller]

Although we disagree with Leppell's claim to have the *best* Twilight merchandise in town—as touted by a sign on their building—they certainly have the largest and most varied selection of Twilight, wolf, and vampire-related souvenirs in a single Forks' store.

Leppell's most legitimate claim to Twilight merchandise fame is their Twi-themed scrapbooking supplies. Charlene stocks a wide variety of Twilight albums, papers, and die cuts. Scrapbookers won't find these items anywhere else in Forks.

Leppell's and Team Forks—Site 8

[©2012 Leppell's photo segment (enhanced)] [*Breaking Dawn Part One* screenshot segment (enhanced)]

Another undeniable Leppell's claim to fame—those wishing to Twi-the-knot in Forks will find no better Twilight **wedding planner** than Leppell's. Charlene's team will handle *everything*: the flower arrangements and Bridal bouquet, tuxedo rental for the Groom and Groomsmen, a garlanded arch and woody furniture similar to those seen in *Breaking Dawn*, and a simulated forest background.

[©2013 CD Miller]

Team Forks Twilight Tours

As mentioned in our Forks-La Push Prologue, Charlene Leppell also operates the Team Forks Twilight Tours company.
http://www.teamforks.com/

Team Forks tours leave from Leppell's store. Children, 10 and younger, tour for half the adult price. Toddlers and lap-riding infants travel for free.

Tour the Twilight Saga Book One

In 2013, Team Forks offered the following Twilight Tour options:
- **A Forks Area Twilight Tour**, 1 ½ hours, $30 per adult
- **A Forks and La Push Twilight Tour**, 3 hours, $40 per adult
- **The "Original" Bella Sunset Tour**, approximately 4 ½ hours, $55 per adult
  This tour is available only by special reservation—weather permitting—with a 6 guest minimum.

> ["If you don't have 6 in your group, call anyway because there may be others hoping to go."]

When Chas and Tara visited in September of 2013, we found Charlene to be a very friendly person. Unfortunately, the Team Forks Twilight tour was not as informative and entertaining—nor as professionally presented—as the **TwiFoot** Twilight tour (Site #12). If the TwiFoot tour is fully booked during your visit, however, the Team Forks tour will fulfill every Twilighter's basic needs. Both tour companies visit the same locations.

[©2013 Tara Miller]

The Team Forks Twilight tour bus carries life-sized cardboard cutouts of Twilight characters to pose with at each location, and provides a stick-on Charlie Swan mustache to wear during your Forks Police Department visit.

Leppell's and Team Forks—Site 8

[©2013 CD Miller]

The only unique Team Forks Twilight tour aspect: after returning to Leppell's, you'll be able to visit the attractions stored in Leppell's private backlot. Charlene has a section of original school lockers salvaged prior to demolition of the old Forks High School, a wedding arch modeled after the one used for filming the Hillywood *Breaking Dawn* parody, and a light-strewn gazebo suggestive of the one seen in *Twilight* prom scenes.

[*Twilight* screenshot segment (enhanced)] [©2013 Tara Miller]

Even though it's installed in a less than picturesque setting, one of the items found in Leppell's backlot is superb. Charlene has the **Casino Monte-Carlo** arch used for shooting *Twilight* prom scenes at **The View Point Inn** in Corbett, Oregon (TTTS Book Three). After filming ended, the arch was either purchased by, or gifted to, the View Point Inn.

Unfortunately, the View Point Inn was gutted by a horrific fire in July of 2011, and had to close, indefinitely. Soon after closure, the inn sold the *Twilight* prom arch to an anonymous collector.

In 2012, Rosemary Colandrea (of TwiFoot tours) negotiated the purchase of the Casino Monte-Carlo arch, for the purpose of including it in the **Twilight Saga Museum** that she, along with Charlene and other local business people, hoped to create in Forks.
http://forksforum.com/news/article.exm/2012-02-15_twilight_museum_concept_detailed_by_chamber_speaker_

Alas, as of 2013, the Forks Twilight Saga Museum plans have foundered and been abandoned. Thus, although it's a rather shabby setting, Leppell's backlot is the closest thing to a Twilight Saga museum that can be found in Forks.

9

Forks Police Department

http://www.forkswashington.org/police-and-corrections
Google Maps & SatNav/GPS: 500 E Division St, Forks, WA 98331
Visit Time: 20 minutes should suffice to snap exterior and interior pix.

ଔଷୋ

[Twilight in Forks screenshot segment (enhanced)]

Forks Police Department, the workplace of Chief Charlie Swan, shares a building with the Forks City Hall, District Courts, and Forks utility departments.

[*Eclipse* screenshot (enhanced)]

The location used for filming Twilight Saga Forks Police Department (FPD) exterior scenes is in **Vernonia, Oregon** (TTTS Book Three), and looks nothing like the real FPD.

[*Twilight* screenshot segment (enhanced)] [©2013 Tara Miller]

Additionally, Forks Police vehicles are white now—not powder blue—and the decals have been redesigned since 2008 *Twilight* filming. But, a real Forks Police Department cruiser is always parked outside the station's building to provide a Twilighter photo op.

Forks Police Department—Site 9

[*Eclipse* screenshot segment (enhanced)] [©2013 CD Miller]

Happily, the 2013 FPD uniform remains the same as the 2008 costume created for **Billy Burke**, including the FPD embroidered arm patch. Wherever you encounter a uniformed Forks Police Officer during your visit, politely ask her or him to pose with you.

[©2013 Matt and Carol Hutchison]

Funny Note: the current Forks Police Chief prefers to wear civilian garb (often a Hawaiian shirt and jeans), rather than a uniform. That's the FPD Chief above, frisking Arkansas Twilighter Matt Hutchison during a special photo op arranged by Nino of **TwiFoot tours** (Site #12) in September of 2013.

Tour the Twilight Saga Book One

[©2013 Tara Miller]

Inside the Forks City Hall building you'll find a glass display cabinet containing some Twilight Saga in Forks photos and memorabilia. (Good luck getting a good shot of it—the glass is *not* non-glare.) Just down the hall is the locked door to the Forks Police Department. If you snap a pic while standing in front of it, be sure not to obstruct the "PO" part of its sign. If you do, you'll be standing in front of the LICE DEPARTMENT door.

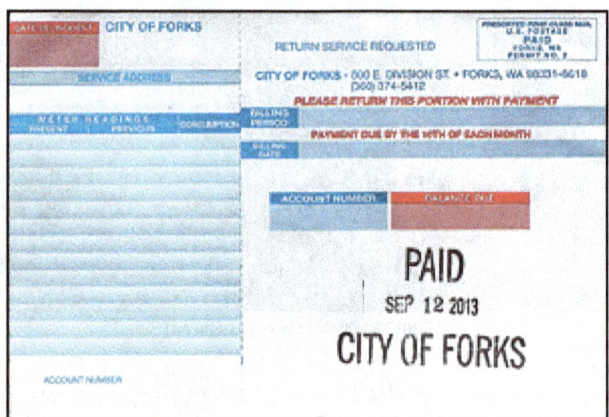

[©2013 CD Miller scanned image]

Before you leave, step inside the Water Department's office. They'll give you a souvenir Forks pen and a date-stamped City of Forks utility bill to commemorate your visit!

10

The Miller Tree Inn

Aka, the Cullen House in Forks
http://millertreeinn.com/
https://www.facebook.com/millertreeinn
http://cullenhouse.blogspot.com/
https://twitter.com/MillerTreeInn

Google Maps & SatNav/GPS: 654 E Division St, Forks, WA 98331

Hours of Operation: This is a private residence and a fully operational B&B. Please do not attempt to enter it unless you'll be lodging here.

Visit Time: Schedule 20 minutes to snap exterior pix as a non-lodger. Those who stay here will have plenty of time to enjoy everything.

ⳇ

[*Twilight* screenshot (enhanced)]

Tour the Twilight Saga Book One

The **Cullen House** exteriors seen on screen were shot on location in **Portland, Oregon** (TTTS Book Three). This home is incredibly beautiful, but it looks *nothing* like the novel's Cullen House description.

> "The trees held their protecting shadow right up to the walls of the house that rose among them, making obsolete the deep porch that wrapped around the first story. The house was timeless, graceful, and probably a hundred years old. It was painted a soft, faded white, three stories tall, rectangular and well proportioned."

Westlands Homestead
[©2013 Tara Miller]

The Cullen House description written by Stephenie Meyer happens to have been inspired by a real-world place—**Westlands Homestead** (Site #23)—only 11 miles north of Forks, with four fabulous vacation cabins for rent.

In 2008, when the Chamber of Commerce developed the first Forks Twilight Tour, however, Westlands Homestead was deemed too far of a trek out of town. So, they searched for an *in-Forks* Cullen House representative, and recognized that the **Miller Tree Inn** came closest to Stephenie's description.

[©2013 CD Miller]

Miller Tree Inn—Site 10

Miller Tree Inn owner/operators, **Bill and Susan Brager**, are two of the most Twilight-friendly folks you'll find anywhere. After recovering from the surprise of their home being designated the Cullen House in Forks, the Bragers embraced the idea and did everything they could think of to enhance the experience of visiting Twilighters.

[©2013 CD Miller]   [Internet-posted photo segment (enhanced), ©unknown]

They began simply enough, by putting the Cullen name on the Miller Tree Inn's mailbox, and mounting a dry-erase board on their front porch, where they posted messages from Esme.

As more and more Twilighters began visiting—both as paying guests and as tourists popping by to take pix of the home's exterior—the Bragers developed additional Twilight Saga attractions within the inn.

[©2013 Tara Miller]

Most notably, Bill and Susan went to a great deal of effort and expense to recreate the **Cullen Graduation Cap Collage** seen on screen, and prominently mounted it in their front room, next to **Edward's Practice Piano**.

Tour the Twilight Saga Book One

[*Twilight* screenshot segment (enhanced)] [*Eclipse* Special Features screenshot segment (enhanced)]

In case there are Twihards tempted to grouse about the inn's Graduation Cap Collage not looking exactly like what was seen in the movies, know that this prop *changed* over the course of Twilight Saga movie filming.

[©2013 CD Miller]

What Makes Bill and Susan Twiliciously Extra-Special?

They invite *non-lodgers* to step up on their front porch!

As long as non-lodgers refrain from entering the house—**Twilighter Treaty!**—you are welcome to putter around on the porch and shoot Twilight Saga feature pix like the one seen above, which was taken through the Miller Tree Inn's front room window. [Put your camera lens right up against the glass to snap the best shot.]

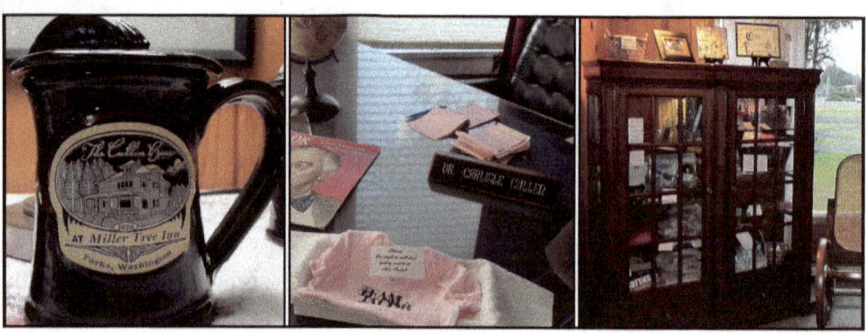

[©2013 CD Miller]

Miller Tree Inn—Site 10

Additional Miller Tree Inn Twilight Saga Attractions Include:

> "…our tables are set with some 'Cullen House' pottery mugs, made especially for us [and available for purchase]. … In the summer of 2011, we added Carlisle's Office, a sitting area on the second floor. Carlisle's Office has some old medical equipment and books and some reproductions of pictures and paintings described in the Twilight book. … Scattered around the front room are a few photographs of the characters … Twilight memorabilia, articles, books, etc."

http://millertreeinn.com/twilight/

> **Side Note:** In 2013, when Stephenie Meyer surprised everyone by making her first appearance at an annual Forks Stephenie Meyer Days celebration, Bill and Susan were thrilled to finally meet her, and gave her one of their unique Cullen House pottery mugs.

We strongly encourage Twilighters to lodge at the Miller Tree Inn on at least one night of an Olympic Peninsula Twilight Saga tour so that you can enjoy access to *all* their attractions, and have plenty of time to enjoy them.

Miller Tree Inn History

[*Destination Forks* screenshot segment (enhanced)]

Erected in 1916, the building has an amazingly Twi-like history. If you lodge here, be sure to ask the Bragers to tell you about the *Forks Doctor with an adopted son* who owned it in the '60s!

Tour the Twilight Saga Book One

[*Destination Forks* screenshot segment (enhanced)]

Bill and Susan bought the property in 1998, and have done their best to maintain the home's historic architecture and charm during renovations designed to improve their guests' comfort.

Each of the eight guestrooms has a modernly-plumbed private bathroom, a mini-fridge stocked with sodas and juice, a satellite TV with DVD player, plenty of electrical outlets, and free Wi-Fi Internet access. Their two-room suites have whirlpool tubs and gas fireplaces. All bookings include a freshly cooked, incredibly delicious, hot breakfast.

To preview the Miller Tree Inn, watch footage shot by Chas and Tara when they lodged here in September of 2013. It's found within our Day One TTTS recon trip video.
http://www.youtube.com/watch?v=NGBvwYqNwmE

🛏 Lodging at Miller Tree Inn

If our endorsement doesn't convince you to lodge here on at least one night of your trip, read the Miller Tree Inn reviews posted by others on **TripAdvisor**.
http://www.tripadvisor.com/Hotel_Review-g58476-d123581-Reviews-Miller_Tree_Inn_Bed_Breakfast-Forks_Washington.html

Before booking a room at the Miller Tree Inn, however, be sure to read the **Westlands Homestead** (Site #23) chapter.

11

Native to Twilight Store

Native American Art and Twilight-Themed Wares
http://www.nativetotwilight.com
https://www.facebook.com/NativeToTwilight
http://forkswa.com/listing/native-to-twilight/

Google Maps & SatNav/GPS: 10 North Forks Avenue, Forks, WA 98331

Open Seven Days a Week: Tourist Season, 9am to 7pm; Off-Season, 10am to 6pm.

Visit Time: Schedule at least 45 minutes to shop here. Team Jacob Twilighters will likely need far longer than that.

☙❧

[©2013 CD Miller]

The **Native to Twilight** store is located on the southwest corner of Forks Avenue and Division Street—the *only* Forks intersection with a stoplight. This store offers a small collection of Twilight-themed vampire and wolf pack clothing and souvenirs, as well as some Forks apparel.

[©2013 CD Miller]

Native to Twilight's specialty, however, is the sale of handcrafted items created by talented **First Nations Artists**. In fact, this is the only place in Forks or La Push where you can be sure that what you're purchasing—whether jewelry or beadwork, pottery or paintings, carvings or wood burnings—was created by native artists.

> "Every craft is authentic. Our gallery collection includes hand-carved cedar canoe paddles by McCarty (Makah Tribe), bent wood cedar boxes by master carver Smith (Quileute and Makah), traditional grass and cedar baskets by Morganroth (Quileute), woven/beaded barrettes by Leitka (Hoh River Tribe), native screen-print designs by Greene (Makah Tribe), and spectacular cedar masks by Taylor (Tulalip) and Cox (Makah Tribe)."

[©2013 CD Miller]

Native to Twilight Store—Site 11

Many of the Native to Twilight products can be previewed by going to their online store, and thus can be purchased electronically from afar.

"All items purchased on this site are shipped directly from Forks."

[©2013 CD Miller]

Chas' favorite Native to Twilight products are their zippered hoodies with screen-printed native totems on the back. Offered in a variety of colors, each color bears a different totem. But, it wasn't until after our trip, that she realized what a special purchase the hoodie seen above turned out to be.

First, we didn't find *zippered* hoodies anywhere else in Forks—or on the Quileute Res. Secondly, the Native to Twilight zip-hoodies with native totems *aren't* offered online.

After further research, we discovered that these hoodies are actually made in **Canada** by the **Native Northwest** company. Happily, that company is equally dedicated to the promotion of First Nations Artists, and its products are only available via reputable brick-and-mortar retailers.
http://nativenorthwest.com

When you travel to Forks, the purchase of a Native Northwest zippered hoodie from Native to Twilight will prove to be a unique Twilight-related personal souvenir or gift.

Tour the Twilight Saga Book One

12

TwiFoot Tours
Twilight Tours in Forks

Vampires, Werewolves, and Bigfoot—*Oh My!*
http://www.twifoottours.com/
http://forkswa.com/listing/twifoot-tours/
https://www.facebook.com/pages/Twifoot-Tours/185906601560399?fref=ts

Hours of Operation: "Always Open!"

Visit Time: Tour times vary—See below

[©2013 Carol & Matt Hutchison]

TwiFoot Tours opened in the spring of 2013. The company is owned and operated by **Nino and Rosemary Colandrea**—two talented Forks Twihards who also happen to be **Squatchers**.
http://www.urbandictionary.com/define.php?term=Squatcher

[©2013 CD Miller]

In addition to a variety of Twilight tours, TwiFoot offers tours of the Olympic Peninsula's **Hoh Rainforest**—with a **Bigfoot** twist. Twilighters with four or more days in the Forks area should do *both* TwiFoot tours.
http://www.olympicpeninsula.org/things-to-do/hoh-rain-forest
http://www.visitolympicpeninsula.org/hoh.html
http://www.olympicproject.com/id18.html
http://www.ptleader.com/news/bigfoot-study-includes-olympic-peninsula-evidence/article_d9a30f64-306d-11e3-b137-0019bb30f31a.html

[©2013 CD Miller]

TwiFoot & Twilight Tours—Site 12

Soon after launching their TwiFoot Tours company, Nino and Rosemary purchased the Twilight tour bus once owned by the **Dazzled by Twilight** company, and took over the **Twilight Tours in Forks** company. This means that TwiFoot always has a back-up bus in case of mechanical difficulties.
http://www.twilighttoursinforkswa.com/
http://www.TourTheTwilightSaga.com/B1/DazzledByTwilightStory.pdf

About the TwiFoot Dynamic Duo

After falling in love with Forks during a visit in 2009, Nino and Rosemary Colandrea—along with their daughter, Jennifer—moved to Forks in 2011, and have been active in the Forks community ever since.

Nino is a retired Police Chief from New York. He worked security for Twilight Saga actors during some of the early filming, as well as during the **2009 TwiCon** in Texas. He's also a non-denominational Minister, who will happily officiate at your Twi-themed wedding in Forks or La Push.

Rosemary is a retired middle school teacher, a member of the original **Stephenie Meyer Days** celebration committee, and was elected President of the Forks **West End Business and Professional Association** in 2013.
http://forkswa.com/listing/west-end-business-and-professional-association/
http://www.stepheniemeyerdays2013.com/
https://www.facebook.com/StephenieMeyerDays2013

[*Twilight* screenshot segment (enhanced)] [©2013 Tara Miller]

Rosemary also is the driving force behind the dream of someday creating a **Twilight Museum** in Forks. In fact, it is largely due to her efforts that the **Casino Monte-Carlo** arch constructed to shoot *Twilight* prom scenes at **The View Point Inn** in Corbett, Oregon (TTTS Book Three) is now in Forks.
http://forksforum.com/news/article.exm/2012-02-15_twilight_museum_concept_detailed_by_chamber_speaker__

Tour the Twilight Saga Book One

Nino drives the TwiFoot bus, keeping his eyes on the road and his mouth respectfully shut during Rosemary's between-site presentations. Once the bus is parked, however, Nino springs to life: providing additional information and performing his special (entirely unpredictable) brand of Twilight shenanigans.

[©2013 CD Miller] [©2013 Tara Miller]

Rosemary is happy to use your camera to capture these unique Nino photo ops for you.

[©2013 CD Miller]

Thanks to their gregarious nature and the degree of respect they've earned during their brief time in Forks, you never know who you might meet while enjoying a TwiFoot Tour with Rosemary and Nino.

TwiFoot & Twilight Tours—Site 12

[©2013 CD Miller]

Tara and Chas were on the TwiFoot tour during Stephenie Meyer's surprise Forks visit on September 13th, 2013. That's Nino and Rosemary in red, above left, arranging to have everyone on their bus taken to the head of the line! You can watch footage of this fabulous treat on Tour the Twilight Saga's YouTube Channel.
http://www.youtube.com/watch?v=XUVc7KOqebg

[©2013 Carol & Matt Hutchison]

Lastly, don't be surprised when the camaraderie inspired by Rosemary and Nino's infectious personalities results in becoming life-long friends with others who share your TwiFoot experience. I know, for a fact, that Chas and Tara of TTTS will forever keep in touch with Carol and Matt from Arkansas.

Tour the Twilight Saga Book One

[Internet-posted photo segment (enhanced), ©unknown]

TwiFoot Tour Schedules

Between October and May, TwiFoot's Twilight Tours are available at 10:30am and 2pm. During the Peak Tourist Season (June through September), an evening Twilight Tour is usually added at 4:30pm ... or 6:30pm ... or *whenever* a group wishes to book one.

Should your schedule require a tour time different from those Nino and Rosemary commonly offer, book in advance and they'll do all they can to accommodate you. If your flight is delayed, or you become stuck in traffic while enroute to Forks, call them.

> "Our times compliment most travelers' schedules, but we also have some flexibility. We completely understand the uncertainty of traffic, so you need NOT drive like a Cullen. We'll work with you as much as possible...all we ask is that you let us know as soon as possible if you are experiencing travel issues."

And, the TwiFoot bus is the only tour bus in town with a wheelchair lift.

TwiFoot Twilight Tour Options in 2013:

- **A Forks Area Twilight Tour**, 1 to 1½ hours, $30 per adult
- **A Deluxe Twilight Tour of Forks and La Push**, 3 to 3½ hours, $40 per adult
- **The Bella Sunset Tour**, approximately 4 to 4½ hours, $55 per adult Tour the town of Forks, then journey to La Push, where you'll enjoy a campfire and picnic supper on the beach, with a spectacular sunset. This tour is available only by special reservation—weather permitting—with a 4 guest minimum.

> ["If you don't have 4 in your group, please call anyway. We may have others waiting for newfound Twilight friends to join them!"]

TwiFoot & Twilight Tours—Site 12

Children 10 years-old and younger can enjoy any of the TwiFoot tours for only $10 each. Infants and toddlers held on the lap of a paying adult travel for free.

Visit the TwiFoot online booking page to view itineraries currently available for each Twilight Tour option, as well as Bigfoot/Hoh Rainforest TwiFoot Tour particulars.
http://www.twifoottours.com/twifoot-toursbook-seats.html

[©2013 CD Miller]

About the TwiFoot Store

During the 2013 season, TwiFoot Tours had a centrally-located storefront and office at 51 North Forks Avenue—a small space sandwiched between the original Dazzled by Twilight (DBT) store, and the burnt-out lot once occupied by the building that housed the second Forks DBT store.

Within their storefront, TwiFoot Tours sold some Twilight Saga and Bigfoot shirts and souvenirs. When her parents were out on a tour, Jennifer kept the store running throughout the day.

In order to diminish TwiFoot's winter operating expenses, however, Nino and Rosemary closed their storefront at the end of September, 2013. But, TwiFoot Tours is still up and running. When driving down the main street in town (Forks Avenue/Hwy 101), you'll see one or both of the TwiFoot busses parked outside their old storefront—which is why the TwiFoot storefront remains on our Forks maps.

Visit **TripAdvisor** to read reviews posted by others.

Tour the Twilight Saga Book One

Twifoot Tours:
http://www.tripadvisor.co.uk/Attraction_Review-g58476-d4227514-Reviews-Twifoot_Tours-Forks_Washington.html

Twilight Tours in Forks
http://www.tripadvisor.co.uk/Attraction_Review-g58476-d2080931-Reviews-Twilight_Tours_in_Forks-Forks_Washington.html

> **Please Note:** Every less-than-excellent review of Twilight Tours in Forks is from the time *before* Nino and Rosemary took over.

13

JT's Sweet Stuffs
JT's Baked Stuffs

"Where Even a Vampire can Satisfy His Sweet Tooth."
http://forkswa.com/listing/jts-sweet-stuffs/
http://forkswa.com/listing/jts-baked-stuffs/

Google Maps & SatNav/GPS: 80 North Forks Avenue, Forks, WA 98331
The Bakery: 86 North Forks Avenue, Forks, WA 98331

Open Seven Days a Week: Peak Season, 10am to 8pm; Off Season, 10am to 6pm.
The Bakery is open daily from 6am to 10am.

Visit Time: Schedule at least 45 minutes for a treat stop and shopping.

Tour the Twilight Saga Book One

[©2013 Tara Miller]

Twiliciously wicked, **JT's Sweet Stuffs** is located just a few doors north of the only stoplight in Forks. Simply reading the Chamber of Commerce website's description will make your mouth water.

> *"The Sweetest Spot in Forks!* Homemade buttery fudge, hand dipped ice cream, saltwater taffy, gourmet chocolates, jelly beans, imported novelty candy, candy containers, sugar free selections. Also featuring soup/sandwiches and gift items."

As their large, iconic ice cream cone sign states, you'll find public rest rooms inside, as well as a Free Wi-Fi signal, making JT's a great place to pop in and sit a spell.

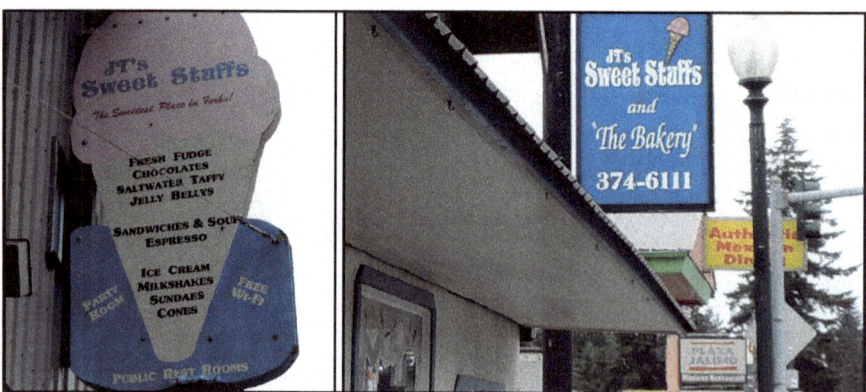

[©2013 Tara Miller]

JT's Sweet Stuffs—Site 13

JT's Baked Stuffs—aka "The Bakery" in Forks

In 2013, Forks residents, **Janet and Tom Hughes** (the names behind "**JT**"), expanded their operation by opening a bakery in the little building located just north of their Sweet Stuffs store. The Bakery opens at 6am each morning, and features freshly baked breads, donuts, pastries, cakes, pies, cupcakes—plus whatever else strikes Janet's fancy that day. If any of the bakery's fresh items remain unsold when it closes at 10am, they're taken to JT's Sweet Stuffs.

[©2013 CD Miller]

Inside JT's you'll find Twilight-themed goodies, as well as several gift items not offered elsewhere. Their inexpensive ($5.99) and adorable Jacob Wolf plush toys are especially irresistible!

JT's Sweet Stuffs is an active member of the Forks business community. Each Wednesday they host the weekly Chamber of Commerce luncheon meeting. And, in 2012, JT's Sweet Stuffs was named Forks Business of the Year for their community-minded activities, such as sponsoring the 11th annual Twinkle Light Holiday Parade.

In 2013, JT's participated with the original **Stephenie Meyer Days** celebration committee by hosting a Breaking Dawn Part 2 Breakfast on Saturday, September 14th, as well as an Ice Cream Social that afternoon.
http://www.stepheniemeyerdays2013.com/stephenie-meyer-days-2013-schedule-of-events.html

Sometime during your Forks visit, you *must* pop into JT's Sweet Stuffs!

Tour the Twilight Saga Book One

14

Sully's Drive-In

Home of the Bella Burger
http://forkswa.com/listing/sullys-drive-in/

Google Maps & SatNav/GPS: 220 North Forks Ave, Forks, WA 98331

Open Monday through Saturday: Tourist Season, 10:30am to 10pm; Off-Season, 10:30am to 9pm.

Visit Time: Plan at least 45 minutes to enjoy a Bella Burger.

[©2013 Tara Miller]

When he didn't have time for a sit-down dinner at Forks Coffee Shop, Chief Charlie Swan often snagged carry-out from **Sully's Drive-In**.

[©2013 CD Miller]

Sully's famous **Bella Burger** is a single beef patty with melted Swiss cheese, lettuce, tomato, and a pineapple slice, sandwiched between buns slathered with a "special sauce." No, we don't know why the Bella Burger is beef, or why it's topped with a pineapple slice. If requested, Sully's will make a *veggie* Bella Burger for you.

Sully's other Twi-themed item is **Twilight Punch**: a clear glass of fresh lemonade on ice, topped with a strawberry and drizzled strawberry syrup. When served, the syrup looks like "blood dripping down" in the glass. Those who order the Bella Burger or Twilight Punch also receive a free set of plastic **Vampire Fangs**!

[©2008 Doug Inglish for *VMan* magazine (enhanced)]

You're right — Twilight Saga vamps don't have fangs. But, if Robert Pattinson can have fun with them, why not us?

Sully's also serves a **Spartan Burger** in honor of the Forks High School athletic teams. This decadent delight consists of a beef patty, melted cheese, lettuce, tomato, a slice of ham, and strips of crispy bacon. If only we were Vampires, and didn't need to worry about cholesterol!

15

Forks Community Hospital

Birthplace of Bella Swan
Dr. Carlisle Cullen's Workplace
http://www.forkshospital.org/
http://wwrhcc.org/forks-community.html
http://forkswa.com/listing/forks-community-hospital/

Google Maps & SatNav/GPS: 530 Bogachiel Way, Forks, WA 98331

Hours of Operation: The Forks Community Hospital is not open to the general public, nor is it a film site. Please do not violate the **Twilighter Treaty** by going inside the hospital, unless you require attention for a legitimate medical condition or emergency.

Visit Time: 20 minutes to snap exterior Dr. Cullen parking sign pix.

Real-World and Twilight Saga Forks Hospital History

The first hospital in Forks was called the **Olympic Clinic**. Built in 1929 by Dr. Ulrick S. Ford—the only doctor in town—it was located at the southwest corner of Forks Avenue and C Street. Dr. Ford and his family lived upstairs until the clinic's increasing space requirements forced them to move.

[*Twilight* Special Features screenshot (enhanced)]

In 1936, when the Cullen family made their treaty with the Quileute Nation, they were living in the Hoquiam area—103 miles south of Forks. Carlisle wasn't working in Forks during that time.
http://www.twilightlexicon.com/the-lexicon/timeline/

Dr. Ford retired in 1947, and Dr. Edwin F. Leibold took over his practice. The Leibold family lived in what is now the **Miller Tree Inn** (Site #10)—aka, the **Cullen House in Forks**. By then, the Olympic Clinic had grown to occupy an entire block, with no more room available for expansion.

In 1948, Thomas Mansfield, a commissioner of Clallam County Hospital District #1, donated a three acre site on Bogachiel Way to the city. The new Olympic Clinic was completed there in November of 1952.

[Internet-posted photo segment (enhanced), ©unknown]

In 1959, the clinic's name was changed to **Forks Community Hospital**. Since then, the hospital has expanded in size several times to meet the area's needs, and it continues to grow. In 2014, a new Forks Community Hospital (FCH) entrance, with a large lobby and waiting room, will be added.

[*Breaking Dawn Part One* screenshot (enhanced)]

Isabella Swan was born in Forks, Washington, on September 13th, 1987. Being the only hospital in town, FCH is Bella's birthplace.

Forks Community Hospital—Site 15

[*Twilight* screenshot (enhanced)]

Carlisle began working at FCH in 2003, when the Cullen clan moved to the Forks area.

Please Note: Emergency room and hospital hallway scenes were shot at a hospital in **Portland, Oregon** (TTTS Book Three).

[Internet-posted photo segment (enhanced), ©unknown, circa 2009] [©2013 CD Miller]

Soon after the *Twilight* tourist surge began, Forks Community Hospital created a Twilicious photo op by reserving a parking space for Dr. Cullen near the emergency department, and posting a sign to identify it. This sign and its location, has changed over the years. We don't know why the sign was redesigned, but it was relocated for an important reason.

Early on the morning of July 7th, 2010, a horrible Coast Guard helicopter crash occurred near James Island at La Push. Three of its four crew members ultimately died.

http://seattletimes.com/html/localnews/2012301842_coptercrash08m.html
http://www.sequimgazette.com/news/article.exm/2010-07-07_helicopter_crash_at_lapush_reported

The first two recovered victims were transported by Forks ambulances—lights flashing and sirens blaring—to Forks Community Hospital. When they arrived, a throng of Twilighters were near the emergency entrance, snapping pix of Dr. Cullen's reserved parking sign. Cameras hot in their hands, several Twilighters took photos of the victims as they were transferred inside. Some of those photos were posted on Facebook pages.

To prevent future patient privacy violations, FCH moved Dr. Cullen's reserved parking place away from the emergency entrance and main hospital building.

[Bing map segment (enhanced), ©2013 Nokia/Microsoft Corp]

Dr. Cullen's reserved parking sign is currently mounted on the **Forks Community Health Resource Center**, a small, L-shaped building located behind Forks Community Hospital—between Bogachiel Way and F Street, off of 5th Avenue. Its location is marked by a red X on the map above.

Both of the Twilight Tour companies in Forks will chauffer you here and give you plenty of time to take pix.

If FCH hosts an event during the annual **Stephenie Meyer Days** celebration—such as the **Blood Drive** held there on September 14th, 2013—Twilighters may be welcomed *inside* the hospital. Please abide by the **Twilighter Treaty**: Do not take photos of anyone you encounter while inside the hospital.

16

The Swan House

Home of Bella and Charlie Swan
Google Maps & SatNav/GPS: 775 K St, Forks, WA 98331
Hours of Operation: This is a private residence, please do not enter it.
Visit Time: 20 minutes to snap exterior pix

[*Twilight* screenshot (enhanced)]

The real-world home used to film *Twilight* exterior scenes of Charlie Swan's house is in **St Helens, Oregon** (TTTS Book Three). For filming Swan House scenes in the other movies, a replica of this house was erected in a small park south of **Vancouver, British Columbia, Canada** (TTTS Book Two).

[*Destination Forks* screenshot (enhanced)]

When the Chamber of Commerce developed the first Twilight Tour of Forks in 2008, Quillayute Valley Schools District educators Kim and David McIrvin volunteered their home to represent the **Swan House**. As one of the few two-story, Craftsman style houses in Forks, it fit the very brief description penned by Stephenie Meyer in *Twilight*.

> "Eventually we made it to Charlie's. He still lived in the small, two-bedroom house that he'd bought with my mother in the early days of their marriage."

[*TiF* segment (enhanced), ©March 20, 2010] [*DF* segment (enhanced), ©December 4, 2010]

To welcome touring Twilighters, the McIrvins installed a **Home of the Swans** sign in their front yard. Unfortunately, the Swan House sign is sometimes

The Swan House—Site 16

stolen. The screenshot segment above left is from *Twilight in Forks*, a DVD released nine months before the *Destination Forks* DVD, source of the screenshot segment above right. Clearly, another sign had been snatched.

[*Destination Forks* screenshot segment (enhanced)] [©2013 Tara Miller]

Because the McIrvins occasionally have to make a new sign, they've installed a donations box. It's Twi-polite to contribute a buck or two when snapping pix here.

[©2013 Tara Miller]

The Swan House is a Private Residence

Please abide by the **Twilighter Treaty**, so that others can continue to enjoy this site long after you've gone.

Do not trespass on private property.
Do not disturb—or photograph—the residents.
Do not bite any humans, for any reason.

Tour the Twilight Saga Book One

17

Russell Road

Where Bella Finds Two Discarded Motorcycles
Google Maps & SatNav/GPS: Russell Road, Forks, WA 98331
Hours of Operation: This is a street in Forks.
Visit Time: 5 minutes to snap street sign pix.

In Chapter 5 of *New Moon*, it's a slow day at Newton's Olympic Outfitters and Mike tells Bella to leave work early. Not wanting to go back to her father's empty house, she aimlessly drives around Forks and ends up stopped on a side street.

> "After a minute … I recognized where I was. I'd parked in the middle of the north lane of Russell Avenue. … in front of the Cheneys' house … across the road lived the Markses."

Suddenly, Bella sees a hand-drawn cardboard sign leaned against the Markses' mailbox post—"FOR SALE, AS IS." Next to it are two rusting and dilapidated motorcycles. When she knocks on the Markses' door, their youngest son answers and gives her both motorcycles, for free.

Tour the Twilight Saga Book One

[Bing map segments (enhanced), ©2013 Nokia/Microsoft Corp]

Russell Road runs between South Forks Avenue (Hwy 101) and Danielson Road, which is about a block north of Bogachiel Way. All private dwellings and businesses found along it are set well back from the road.

😠Russell Road is Assigned a Might-be-Fun Rating Because:
- There are no Cheneys or Markses mailboxes on Russell Road.
- This event wasn't filmed for the movie—there are no Russell Road screenshots.

[©2013 CD Miller]

Twilighters will be happy snapping street sign post pix through a Forks Twilight Tour Bus window when approaching Russell Road after leaving the **Swan House** (Site #16) on K Street, while enroute to the **Forks Chamber of Commerce** (Site #4). If you ask, the bus will even stop and wait while you step out to take a few Russell Road street sign pix.

Twihards divinely inspired to visit Russell Road independently should first find an empty cardboard box, make a "FOR SALE, AS IS" sign, and take it with them to lean against a Russell Road street sign. Please properly dispose of your prop when finished with it.

18

Old Mill Trading Post & the Round House

The 110 Industrial Park
Shopping and Special Events
http://www.110industrialpark.com/
http://forkswa.com/listing/110-business-park/

Google Maps & SatNav/GPS: 100 La Push Road, Forks, WA 98331

Store Hours of Operation: Tourist Season, Monday-Friday 10:30am to 5:30pm; Saturday 10am to 5:30pm; Sunday 10am to 5pm. Off-Season, Monday-Saturday 10:30am to 5 pm; Sunday 11am to 5pm.

Visit Time: Plan at least 45 minutes to shop and shop and shop.

08&0

Back when Forks was known as the Logging Capital of the World, a large lumber mill operated on the corner of Hwy 101 and Hwy 110 (La Push Road). Owned by different companies over the years, the sawmill finally closed in 1997 and the site was abandoned. In 2008 the entire property, with all its dilapidated buildings and rusting equipment, was purchased by Bill and Kitty Sperry, who have transformed it into the **110 Industrial Park**—a diverse collection of local businesses. In addition to two stores, it currently

Tour the Twilight Saga Book One

includes a small conference center, artisan workshops, storage rental units, propane sales, U-Haul rentals, and an archery range.

[©2013 Tara Miller]

The Old Mill Trading Post
https://www.facebook.com/pages/Old-Mill-Trading-Post/102733993127834
http://forkswa.com/listing/old-mill-trading-post/

Located at the Hwy 110 entrance, the Old Mill Trading Post is the Industrial Park's anchor store. It opened in 2010, and occupies the largest renovated sawmill building. Inside you'll find a dizzying display of locally hand-crafted gifts and gourmet foods, Native American art and jewelry, Twi-themed things such as dream catchers, as well as rooms crammed full of area antiques.

[©2013 CD Miller]

Old Mill Trading Post & the Round House—Site 18

[©2013 CD Miller]

Décor d' Forks
http://forkswa.com/listing/decor-d-forks/

Another noteworthy store found within the 110 Industrial Park, Décor d' Forks is located in Building 7. It opens every morning at 11am, and closes at 3pm Monday through Friday, 5pm on Saturday, 4pm on Sunday. Warning: there are wonderful things here!

[©2013 CD Miller]

As described on its Forks COC webpage:

> "Purveyor of Handcrafted Home Enhancements, Decor d' Forks specializes in hand-crafted items made by local artists. Rustic wood furniture, yard art, hand-carved canes and sculptures are some of the items they carry. 'When folks create things just because they enjoy doing it, you get a quality unmatched by anything mass-produced.'"

[©2008 110 Industrial Park]

The Round House

The Round House was the sawmill's central hub of operation. An open-sided shelter constructed of old growth red cedar, the Round House contained a gigantic, revolving round table used to sort lumber. In 2009, the Sperrys began to carefully transform this historic structure into a full-service community event center.

[©2008 110 Industrial Park] [©2009 110 Industrial Park]

After dismantling the gears and support system, the round sorting table was gently lowered to the ground, then tastefully augmented to become a circular dance floor.

Old Mill Trading Post & the Round House—Site 18

[©2013 CD Miller]

After being walled-in to protect event attendees from the weather, renovation of the **Round House Planner Building** was completed in 2011.

Special Events are Frequently Held in the Round House

Many of these events are free. When an admission fee is charged, it's rarely more than $10 and the proceeds are almost always donated to a local charity or community cause. Below are examples of recent Round House events.

- November 10th, 2012: The 18th Annual Wine & Cheese Hoh Down, sponsored by the Forks COC, to benefit the Visitor Information Center—$10 entry fee.
- June 22nd, 2013: Live Music, Food and Beer Garden, to benefit the Tod Horton Memorial—$10 entry fee.
- July 27-29, 2013: The 1st Annual Forks Woodcrafters Jamboree, sponsored by Décor d' Forks. This event featured local woodworkers and artisans, several area food vendors, door prizes, raffles, carnival games, and a diverse mix of live entertainment. No entry fee was charged, however donations were encouraged and benefited the local Woodcrafters Association.
- During the **Stephenie Meyer Days** celebration in September, 2013, a Forks Music Festival was held at the Round House on the evening of Bella's birthday. Featuring local entertainers from Forks and the Res, celebration guests Hilly and Hannah Hindi of the Hillywood Show also performed. No entry fee was charged, however donations were encouraged to offset expenses incurred by the event host, the Forks Police Department.

When planning your Twilight Saga sojourn, go to the Forks Chamber of Commerce Upcoming Events webpage to learn what is scheduled at the Round House—and elsewhere in Forks—during your visit.
http://forkswa.com/events/

Tour the Twilight Saga Book One

[©2013 CD Miller]

Special Note: The Old Mill Trading Post is a great place to buy inexpensive firewood for your La Push First Beach bonfire.

19

Three Rivers Resort

The Quileute Nation Treaty Line
http://www.threeriversresortandguideservice.com/
https://www.facebook.com/pages/Three-Rivers-Resort-Strictly-Fishing/297060530316412
http://threeriversresort.wordpress.com/

Google Maps & SatNav/GPS: 7765 LaPush Road, Forks, WA 98331
Coordinates for Bing Maps: 47.912833,-124.534625

Groceries, Gas, & Restaurant Hours: Summer, 8am to 9pm; Winter, 9am to 7pm.

Visit Time: 20 minutes to snap exterior sign pix, 45 or more minutes to also enjoy the shop and restaurant.

Tour the Twilight Saga Book One

[Segment (enhanced), map of the Indian nations and tribes of the territory of Washington, circa 1857, ©University of WA Libraries Manuscripts, Special Collections, University Archives Division]

An historic treaty line actually exists on La Push Road, between Forks and the Quileute Reservation. This line marks the boundary between Quileute land and land they surrendered to white settlers, based on an 1856 treaty with the United States government.
http://content.lib.washington.edu/curriculumpackets/treaties/quileutetreaty.html

It wasn't until many years later that the Quileute Nation realized they'd been tricked. In 1872, the Washington Territory superintendent of Indian Affairs reported the Quileutes' complaints in his annual report to the commissioner of US Indian Affairs:

> "The Quileutes ... say they never agreed to sell their country, nor did they, to their knowledge, sign any treaty disposing of their right to it. That they were present at the time the treaty with them is alleged to have been made, but that the paper they signed was explained to them to be an agreement to keep the peace with citizens of the United States, and to accord them the same rights to come into their country and trade for furs, etc. as had previously been accorded to the Hudson Bay Company..."

http://content.lib.washington.edu/curriculumpackets/treaties/quileutestay.html

While the Quileutes refused to recognize the false land treaty, they continued to honor the agreement they believed was made in 1856. They were always described as accommodating and peaceable when dealing with white settlers who frequently infringed upon their land. It likely was the Quileutes' peaceful nature of persistent resistance that led to their ultimate success in retaining possession of *some* of their ancient tribal territories.

Three Rivers Resort—Site 19

> "Not unexpectedly, some white settlers sought to deprive the local Native Americans of the tiny fragments of the homelands the Indians had been allowed to retain after the treaties were approved. What is more surprising is that the Quileute, Makah, and the Hoh found ready allies among some of the federal officials. Through a steadfast refusal to surrender to white pressure, the three tribes eventually succeeded in holding on to their remaining lands and establishing reservations that their descendants still call home."

http://content.lib.washington.edu/curriculumpackets/treaties/conclusion.html

Happily, Stephenie Meyer's Twilight Saga has helped transform the La Push Road Quileute treaty line from a shameful example of the U.S. government's historic mistreatment of indigenous peoples, to a harmlessly fun photo op that represents absolutely *no* disrespect for the Quileute Nation. To ensure that future Twilighters are allowed to enjoy the Treaty Line—and other Quileute Reservation locations—please be respectful of Quileute people wherever you encounter them, whether or not you're a member of Team Jacob!

[©2013 CD Miller]

The **Three Rivers Resort** grocery store and gas station straddles the historic Quileute Treaty Line on La Push Road. Prior to the *Twilight* tourism surge, however, **no sign** marked the treaty line's location.

Tour the Twilight Saga Book One

[*Destination Forks* screenshot segments (enhanced)]

Sometime after *New Moon* was published in 2006, Three Rivers Resort erected a double-sided Treaty Line Sign to welcome Twilight Saga fans. The original two signs have periodically been replaced by more elaborate versions over the years. Above is how the signs appeared in 2010.

[©2013 Tara Miller]

Above, are the Treaty Line signs present in September of 2013.

[©2013 Tara Miller]

Three Rivers Resort—Site 19

Two other Twilicious sign photo ops are also found outside Three Rivers Resort. Both Forks-based Twilight Tour busses make a short stop here to allow time for exterior sign pic snapping.

Please Note: The Vampire Threat Level is based on the amount of sun shining through the forest canopy on any given day. Bright and sunny, cloudless conditions: Vampire Threat Level LOW.

[©2013 CD Miller]

To enjoy the grocery and gift store (above), or the restaurant (below), you'll need to visit the Three Rivers Resort on your own.

[©2013 Tara Miller] [©2013 Three Rivers Resort]

And, yes! The Three Rivers Restaurant offers delectable Twi-themed dishes, as well as a reserved Twilighter seating area.

Twilighters can preview the Three Rivers grocery and restaurant online.
http://www.threeriversresortandguideservice.com/

[Internet-posted Three Rivers Resort photo, ©unknown]

🛏 Lodging at Three Rivers Resort

If your Twilight Saga touring party consists of 3 to 6 people—and the **Cabins at Beaver Creek** (Site #23) are fully booked—consider staying in a Three Rivers Resort cabin.

> "Each of our cabins are 1 or 2 beds with private baths and include the following: Full Size Refrigerator, Stove with Oven, Microwave and Toaster, Coffee Pot, Cooking Utensils, Direct TV, Alarm Clock, Free Wifi. Pets Welcome with Fee."

http://www.threeriversresortandguideservice.com/Cabins.html

Camping Twilighters will thoroughly enjoy the many amenities available at Three Rivers Resort's RV Park and camp ground.
http://www.threeriversresortandguideservice.com/campground.html

20

Jacob Black's House
The Wolf Den

Twi-Themed Vacation Rental Properties on La Push Road

Hours of Operation: These are private dwellings. Please do not trespass on the porch unless you've booked a room.

Visit Time: 30 minutes is plenty to snap exterior pix at both sites.

[©2013 CD Miller]

Tour the Twilight Saga Book One

The distinctive home and outbuildings used to shoot scenes at Billy and Jacob Black's house still exist. This property is located northeast of Vancouver, British Columbia, Canada, in **Coquitlam** (TTTS Book Two). While visiting the Olympic Peninsula, however, you'll find its look-alike on the road between Forks and La Push.

La Push Road cottage above left—Coquitlam cottage above right
[©2013 Tara Miller] [©2013 CD Miller]

Jacob Black's House
http://www.jacobblackshouse.com/
http://forkswa.com/listing/jacob-blacks-house-vacation-rental/

Google Maps & SatNav/GPS: 8320 La Push Road, Forks, WA 98331

When Linda Middleton learned that Twilighters thought her family's home looked a little like the Billy and Jacob Black house seen in the movies, she turned it into a Twi-themed vacation rental property.

> "With the help of her husband and sons, Middleton began transforming each room in her home to reflect the look and feel of the film. She hand painted murals in one bedroom with trees. She also cut up old pairs of her son's jeans and left pieces strewn throughout the home as if Jacob had suddenly transformed into a werewolf right there in the living room."

http://news.yahoo.com/blogs/abc-blogs/twilight-getaway-vacation-rental-home-offers-movie-inspired-160336626--abc-news-travel.html

La Push Road barn above left—Coquitlam barn above right
[©2013 Tara Miller] [©2013 CD Miller]

Jacob Black's House & The Wolf Den—Site 20

In 2009, Jacob Black's House on La Push Road caught the eye of Hilly and Hannah Hindi—aka **The Hillywood Show**—and Middleton granted them permission to film portions of their *New Moon Parody* on the property. Oddly enough, only a tiny corner of the cottage appears in the video. The glimpses of parody-Jacob's home feature the ground floor of the Middleton's barn and some outbuildings—structures that look nothing like the Twilight Saga film site.
http://www.youtube.com/watch?v=ti13oOYvyp8

[*New Moon Parody* screenshot segments (enhanced) above and below, ©2010 The Hillywood Show]

Tour the Twilight Saga Book One

[*Destination Forks* screenshot segment (enhanced)] [©2013 Tara Miller]

Jacob Black's House is located less than a mile west of the **Treaty Line Sign** (Site #19). Because it is a private residence and vacation rental property, it is important to observe the **Twilighter Treaty** while visiting. Happily, the Middletons created exterior features for non-lodging Twilighters to snap pix of, and both Forks-based Twilight Tour companies stop here. According to Nino Colandrea of **TwiFoot Tours**, there always is a motorcycle chained to the "B BLACK" mailbox.

> "You can sit on the motorcycle for photos, and walk in the front yard to take pictures of the Jacob Black sign and the house. But, you need to stay off the porch and away from the windows."

Finding reviews of the accommodations offered here is strangely difficult. Jacob Black's House was not listed on **TripAdvisor** in 2013. After hours of hunting, we found three reviews on two other websites.
http://www.yelp.com/biz/jacob-black-house-forks

10/21/2013:

> "We rented one bedroom in Apartment B. The room was small and shabby but okay to sleep. However, when I checked my credit card bill I was actually charged $25 more than agreed. I inquired, but I was told [it was] because we used the bathroom! I was shocked. Giving a room on rent but not allowed to use the bathroom? We did not even use the shower! The owner was not a nice woman … I would not suggest anyone to stay in this house. If you are a fan of the movie, drive by and take the picture is enough, there are much better places to stay."

Jacob Black's House & The Wolf Den—Site 20

08/26/2012:

"This was a perfect rustic rental house for our party of 10 (half were kids ages 2-8). Adorable Twilight theme, great space, relaxing environment. LOVED the outdoor fire pit and tree swing. The only drawback was the electric cow fence on the property. We spent a lot of effort keeping the kids away from it. Beware the offer of free s'mores—they only provide supplies for exactly four s'mores."

http://www.flipkey.com/forks-farmhouse-rentals/p390167/

Posted on 06/10/2012 for a stay in July 2011:

"This place is seriously one of the best places I've ever stayed at! The moment I walked through that door I thought I was home! I would stay here again in a heartbeat!"

[©2013 Tara Miller]

The Wolf Den
http://www.wolfdencabinrental.com/
http://forkswa.com/listing/wolf-den-cabin-rental/

Google Maps & SatNav/GPS: 8343 La Push Road, Forks, WA 98331

The Wolf Den vacation rental cabin is across the street and half a block west of Jacob Black's House. Twilight Tour busses also stop here.

[©2013 CD Miller] [©2013 Tara Miller]

This lovely log home looks nothing like the novel description of Sam and Emily's forest cottage, nor the *New Moon* film set. But, it's easy to imagine teenaged Quileutes finding sanctuary here while learning to control newly-acquired wolf powers.

Non-lodging Twilighters are welcome to snap pix of the Wolf Den sign, the interesting front yard findings, and the log home. The cabin's porch and interior, however, are strictly off-limits.

Like Jacob Black's House, the Wolf Den didn't have a **TripAdvisor** listing in 2013. Elsewhere, however, we found a site that offers a multitude of reviews, in addition to several photos of interior rooms—including the Jacuzzi and the laundry.
http://www.homeaway.com/vacation-rental/p296927

Of the twenty-two Home Away reviews posted about Wolf Den stays between July of 2010 and June of 2013, twenty gave it the maximum Five-Star rating. The two Four-Star-rated reviews didn't contain any complaints.

21

La Push First Beach

Jacob & Bella's Beach
(Bella's Tide Pools)
http://www.forks-web.com/fg/beach123.htm
http://forkswa.com/first-beach-webcam/
http://en.wikipedia.org/wiki/La_Push_Beach

Google Maps: First Beach, La Push, WA
SatNav/GPS coordinates and driving directions provided below.

★**View Quileute Country Etiquette Before Visiting:**
http://www.quileutenation.org/indian-country-etiquette

Hours of Operation: Open to the public 24/7.

Visit Time: Both Forks-based Twilight Tour companies offer bus trips that make a brief photo op stop at First Beach. However, no less than **one hour** is required to fully enjoy a Twilicious "*La Push-Baby*" beach visit. Schedule at least **three additional hours** for a *Twilight* tide pool trek.

Tour the Twilight Saga Book One

[©2013 Tara Miller]

Of the three **La Push** beaches—First, Second, and Third—**First Beach** is the primary Twilight Saga novel setting. One mile long and crescent-shaped, First Beach is a combination of two beach types. A thin strip of fine sand stretches between the water's edge and a wide stone beach liberally strewn with driftwood logs of all sizes, each bleached almost bone-white by the salt waves—exactly as Stephenie Meyer described it in *Twilight*.

Seagulls, eagles, and seals are seen here year-round. March, April, and May are the best months for migratory whale-watching.
http://thewhaletrail.org/la-push-2
http://www.peninsuladailynews.com/article/20100326/news/303269992

Surfers and kayakers of all experience levels also flock to First Beach year-round.
http://www.wannasurf.com/spot/North_America/USA/North_West/Washington/la_push/
http://solspot.com/la-push-surf-report/
http://magicseaweed.com/La-Push-Surf-Report/308/

According to *Twilight: Director's Notebook*, when she scouted Forks and La Push hoping to film at the real-world locations in Stephenie's novel, Catherine Hardwicke described First Beach as being "drop-dead gorgeous." Unfortunately, Washington State filming fees in 2008 proved too expensive for the first movie's small budget. Thus, Hardwicke had to shoot *Twilight*'s La Push beach scenes at **Indian Beach** in **Ecola State Park, Oregon** (TTTS Book Three).
http://www.amazon.com/Twilight-Directors-Notebook-Story-Stephenie/dp/B005UVR9N0

La Push First Beach—Site 21

[*Twilight* screenshot (enhanced)]

Indian Beach *Twilight* footage includes van-side parking lot action, as well as Jacob and Bella walking on the beach while he tells her about Quileute legends involving the tribe's wolf origins and the mysterious cold ones.

[*New Moon* screenshot (enhanced)]

Scenes of Bella and Jacob discussing his werewolf condition in *New Moon* were also shot at Indian Beach.

Happily, Indian Beach was selected as a substitute because it looks a lot like First Beach. Thus, Twilighters can snap similar screenshot recreations of the *Twilight* and *New Moon* scenes above when visiting the novel's real-world beach.

Tour the Twilight Saga Book One

[©2013 Tara Miller]

Prominently seen at the north end of First Beach is **James Island**—called **A-ka-lat** by the Quileutes, meaning Top of the Rock. James Island guards the mouth of the Quillayute River, and is significant in Quileute culture both as a source of spirit power and as the burial place of high-status tribal members for hundreds of years.
http://www.quileutenation.org/culture/history
http://en.wikipedia.org/wiki/Quillayute_River
http://en.wikipedia.org/wiki/James_Island_%28Washington%29
http://forkswa.com/james-island-webcam/

[©2013 Tara Miller]

Dogs on the Beach

First Beach is the only La Push beach where dogs are allowed. Although a leash law is in effect here, we noticed that locals seem to ignore it. Whether or not you keep your dog on a leash, please be sure to bag and pack out everything you—*or your dog*—bring to the beach.

La Push First Beach—Site 21

Rialto Beach begins on the north side of the Quileute River, but it isn't a La Push Beach. Rialto Beach is part of the Olympic National Park, and leashed dogs are allowed there as far north as Ellen Creek. Because Ellen Creek is only half-way to Rialto's tide pools, you cannot take your pooch tidepooling (more info below).

The **Washington Trails Association** has a webpage with answers to many hiking-with-dogs FAQ, as well as important tips for ensuring the health and safety of your Twi-trek canine companion.
http://www.wta.org/hiking-info/basics/hiking-with-dogs

[Internet-posted photo segment (enhanced), ©2013 Chelsea Nichole]

Campfires on the Beach

Twilighters who book a **Bella's Sunset Tour** with the TwiFoot or Team Forks companies can enjoy a First Beach campfire without having to lift a finger. To build your own First beach campfire:

- **BYOF—Bring Your Own Firewood.** Burning beach driftwood is against tribal law. Firewood bundles are sold at the **Forks Thriftway** (Site #5), the **Three Rivers Resort** store (Site #19), and the **Lonesome Creek** store (info in Site #22). The cheapest and most convenient place to buy firewood, however, is the **Old Mill Trading Post** (Site #18).
- **Purchase a Beach Fire Permit.** Available only at the **Quileute Oceanside Resort** office (info in Site #22), the permit is inexpensive—$5 in 2013.
- **Bring a bucket with you.** If not properly extinguished, beach campfires pose significant danger to other visitors, as well as to delicate marine life. Covering a campfire with sand extinguishes the flames, but locks in the heat. Sand-covered coals can continue to smolder for 24 hours or more. Since they cannot be seen, sand-

Tour the Twilight Saga Book One

covered coals are extremely dangerous to children who might see your stone-circled fire pit as a sandbox divine for digging. To properly extinguish a beach campfire:

Drench your fire pit with several buckets of seawater.
Stir it with a driftwood staff.
Wait 5 to 10 minutes, then drench and stir again.

🚗 Going to First Beach

There are three points from which to visit First Beach. Twilight Tour busses will take you to one of them. The other two can only be enjoyed by Twilighters who visit independently.

[Bing map segments (enhanced), ©2013 Nokia/Microsoft Corp]

Point A

Parking Lot SatNav/GPS Coordinates: 47.898211,-124.624219

When approaching from the east (Forks), you'll see the Second Beach parking lots just before reaching the bend where La Push Road curves north — the red X above. Park there and follow the paved pedestrian path next to the road until you reach Point A: the **First Beach Viewing Platform**.

[©2013 Tara Miller]

La Push First Beach—Site 21

Point A's platform offers stunning views of James Island and the ocean vista beyond. When armed with binoculars, this elevated site is the best place for migratory whale watching in March, April, and May.

[©2013 CD Miller]

A **Tsunami evacuation trail** is maintained between the viewpoint platform and the south end of First Beach. The trail is slippery when wet—almost always—but it's short and only slightly steep in places. Twilighters wearing sturdy shoes will thoroughly enjoy this trek.

[©2013 Tara Miller]

The south end of First Beach is rumored to be the best place to find **sea glass**—broken glass that has been tumbled against the sand by sea waves, smoothing and polishing its edges.
http://en.wikipedia.org/wiki/Sea_glass

Tour the Twilight Saga Book One

[©2008 Norsk Bokmal]

According to a local resident, broken glass found on the beach is technically *garbage*. As such, it is not subject to Res Ordinance 74-A-8, which prohibits removal of objects or artifacts from any La Push beach. In fact, you are doing your duty as an eco-conscious visitor by removing garbage from the beach. In the unlikely event that someone confronts you about collecting sea glass, that's your story. Stick to it.

[Bing map segments (enhanced), ©2013 Nokia/Microsoft Corp]

Point B

Store SatNav/GPS Coordinates: 47.904232,-124.629618

The easiest First Beach access—especially for mobility-limited Twilighters—is found behind the only grocery store on the Res, **Lonesome Creek** (info in Site #22). This is where Twilight Tour busses stop. The parking lot is right at the edge of the rock beach and visitors can reach the sand by walking around, rather than climbing over, the piles of giant driftwood logs.

La Push First Beach—Site 21

North End of First Beach as Seen from Point B
[©2013 Tara Miller]

Almost exactly in the middle of First Beach, Point B is slightly more than a half-mile hike from the north end, a little less than a half-mile from the south end. When visiting via tour bus, however, you'll not have enough time to reach either end. Happily, you can snap distant views of the entire beach from this central location.

South End of First Beach as Seen from Point B
[©2013 Tara Miller]

Twilighters who don't mind a two-mile beach trek (don't forget the return hike from each end) can visit *all* of First Beach after parking at the Point B car park.

Tour the Twilight Saga Book One

[Bing map segments (enhanced), ©2013 Nokia/Microsoft Corp]

Point C

Parking Lot SatNav/GPS Coordinates: 47.908245,-124.63981

Address Alternative (the **River's Edge Restaurant**, info in Site #22):
41 Main Street, La Push, WA 98305

[©2013 Tara Miller]

Point C is a gravel parking lot with close-up views of James Island and quick access to the north end of First Beach. Go to Point C by continuing north on La Push Road, past the Lonesome Creek store and Quileute Oceanside Resort, until you reach the old **La Push Village** (info in Site #22).

La Push First Beach—Site 21

[©2013 Tara Miller]

La Push Road/Ocean Front Drive ends when it becomes Coast Guard Road—at the zebra-crossing seen above, flanked by a "NO THRU Traffic" sign. There, the main road leads you to the right, onto Alder Street.

Once on Alder Street, take the next left and drive north on River Street. At the end of River Street, turn left—a right turn leads east to the River's Edge Restaurant.

[©2013 CD Miller]

Follow the road as it twists west from River Street until you see the Point C gravel parking lot with James Island perched beyond it. This old La Push Village area is called **The Point**. Head left and park in a spot closest to the car park's south side.

There is no fee for automobile parking at The Point.

According to our local guide, however, during special Quileute events you may be approached by a native individual asking you to pay her/him for parking. Should that happen, *just pay them*. They'll not ask for more than a buck or two, because they aren't sanctioned by the Quileute Council and won't want to generate complaints.

[Bing map segment (enhanced), ©2013 Nokia/Microsoft Corp]

There are four access paths at the north end of First Beach:

- An unmarked, rough path leads to the beach from the southeastern corner of The Point's car park.
- To reach a fairly smooth path, walk east from the car park, along the one-way drive in front of **Jacob's High School** (info in Site #22), until you reach the corner where the drive curves left and heads to the school. The "no admittance" sign seen here applies to automobile traffic on the drive, *not* pedestrian use of the footpath to First Beach.
- As seen in aerial maps, there are two additional beach access paths along the dirt drive that stretches between the High School road and the northwestern border of Quileute Oceanside Resort.

[©2013 CD Miller]

The unmarked path at The Point's southeast corner is a short stretch of several rough and uneven steps. When you arrive at the rock beach, you must climb over tangled piles of driftwood logs to reach the sand. As the shortest route between beach and car park, this path is often used by surfers.

[©2013 CD Miller]

The beach-side entrance to this path is also **unmarked** (above, center). While you could memorize a driftwood landmark to find The Point's path when returning to your car, it's a better idea to walk a little further south and exit First Beach via the **signed** access path.

[©2013 CD Miller]

We call the path between the High School drive and First Beach a signed path because of its beach-side "**Trail**" sign. This access path is much smoother and easier to walk than The Point's path, and there are fewer logs to climb over. Even if you entered from The Point, by leaving First Beach via this path you can snap Jacob High School pix on the way back to your car.

[©2013 CD Miller]

Twilight Tide Pools

From *Twilight*:

> "I loved the tide pools. They had fascinated me since I was a child; they were one of the only things I ever looked forward to when I had to come to Forks."

Alas, you'll not find tide pools at First Beach. To experience the tide pools that inspired Stephenie Meyer, you'll need to visit the Olympic National Park's **Rialto Beach** or La Push's **Second Beach**.

What are Tide Pools?

Tide pools are rocky pockets of ocean shoreline entirely submerged by seawater when the tide is high, and almost completely drained when the tide goes out.
http://en.wikipedia.org/wiki/Tide_pool
http://www.visitolympicpeninsula.org/tidepools.html

Tide pools are fascinating because more than 300 species of unusually shaped, often brilliantly colored, aquatic creatures and plants live in them — magical marine inhabitants only visible when visiting a continent's shore during low tide.

Throughout the millennia, tide pool organisms have evolved and adapted to survive the violent forces of wind, wave, and current that routinely

La Push First Beach—Site 21

batter the coastline. Unfortunately, tide pool creatures and plants remain extremely vulnerable to human incursion. The damage caused by a single misstep may take a tide pool *years* to recover.

It is vitally important that Twilighters show extreme care and respect for tide pool inhabitants when trekking to view them. Please go to both the links below and learn about **Tide Pool Etiquette** before your tide pool visit.
http://olympiccoast.noaa.gov/living/habitats/intertidal/ettiquette.html
http://oregontidepools.org/etiquette

Highlights from the Tide Pool Etiquette Links Above:

- Bring a bag with you on every beach outing. Pick up any paper, glass, metal or plastic trash that you find, and take it away when you leave—along with anything you brought with you.
- While working your way out to the farthest-from-shore tide pools, step only on bare rock—for your safety as well as that of the tide pool inhabitants. Exposed wet rocks are far less slippery than rocks that remain submerged. More importantly, stepping *into* a tide pool can cause catastrophic injury to the creatures that live there.
- It is helpful to use a driftwood walking stick when traversing the beach. But, please leave your stick on the beach when trekking out to tide pools. Thrusting a walking stick tip into a tide pool will cause damage.
- **"If you pry, it will die."**
Creatures who dwell in tide pools survive the forces of wind, wave, and current by firmly attaching themselves to rocks. Feel free to gently *touch* tide pool creatures, but **do not attempt to pick them up**. Prying a tide pool inhabitant from its rock squeezes its internal organs and rips-off sections of its suckers (feet). Any creature pried up will likely die after you've admired it.

Inhabitants of the Best Rialto and Second Beach Tide Pools:

- Purple, red, and yellow starfish
- Green and pink sea anemones
- Spiny sea urchins
- Hard-shelled snails, limpets, barnacles, and crabs

Several varieties of algae, kelp, and seaweed are spied in every Olympic Peninsula tide pool—even those close to shore.

Tour the Twilight Saga Tidepooling Tips

Twilighters with time for tidepooling can find additional information and visiting tips vital to tide pool trip planning in a PDF we created and posted on our website. This guide includes the following subjects:

Tour the Twilight Saga Book One

- How Do You Find the Best Tide Pools?
- How Fast Does the Tide Come Back In?
- Tide Pool Visit Planning Tips
- Footwear for Tidepooling
- Cameras and Tide Pools

http://www.TourTheTwilightSaga.com/B1/21TidePoolTips.pdf

Tour the Twilight Saga Prefers Rialto Beach Tide Pools

Chas and Tara visited Second Beach tide pools during our September 2013 recon trip, but didn't have time to also schedule a Rialto Beach tide pools visit. After our Second Beach experience we interviewed several locals and other visitors about Rialto Beach, and wished we'd gone there instead.

Second Beach car park enroute to First Beach—Second Beach car park on the way back to Forks.
[©2013 Tara Miller]

Second Beach (SB) is the tide pool haven closest to First Beach. Its car parks are located *on* the route between Forks and First Beach, at the bend in La Push Road. Reaching SB involves a 20 to 30 minute rain forest hike, followed by a 20 minute beach walk to the nearest tide pool area. It sounds so quick and pleasant. It is not.

Although it's extremely beautiful, the forest trail between SB car parks and beach is arduous and entirely unsuitable for visitors in less-than-robust health—especially the Death Climb that begins the return hike. Reviewers who call this trek easy must be accustomed to frequent hiking and steep, uneven step-climbing. Twilighters who have any manner of mobility difficulties should stay away from Second Beach.

La Push First Beach—Site 21

[©2013 John Simpson of Cabins at Beaver Creek (Site #23)]

Rialto Beach (RB) is a section of shoreline that stretches north from where the Quileute River spills into the Pacific Ocean. Although RB lies directly across the river from the north end of First Beach (and the old La Push Village), you cannot cross to the Quileute River's northern bank at its mouth. Happily, it's only a 5-mile side trip off of La Push Road to reach the RB car parks found at the end of **Mora Road**—car parks that are practically *on* the beach

At Rialto you usually can walk *around* the giant driftwood log piles to reach the sand beach. (Log piles at SB must be climbed *over*.) As part of the Olympic National Park, RB also has well maintained toilet facilities that are **clean**, and running water is available for hand washing—a far cry from the horrific privy found at SB!

A few reviewers complain that the hour-long, rocky-sand trek to Rialto's tide pool area is sloggy and somewhat difficult in places. Even if that's occasionally true, the sloggiest RB beach walk is far less arduous than the Death Climb at SB.

There is one tricky bit on the trek to RB's tide pools—a small creek crossing. Those fearful of using wide driftwood logs to cross, however, can wade through the shallow water at the mouth of the creek.

Second Beach Tide Pool
[©2013 Tara Miller]

Bottom Line: There are fascinating tide pools at *both* SB and RB, but Rialto's are far more easily accessed. For Twilighters who prefer to learn more, we created a **TwiTips** PDF containing additional information about both beaches, including Internet research links and photos.
http://www.TourTheTwilightSaga.com/B1/21RSBeaches.pdf

[©2013 Tara Miller]

🚗 Going to Rialto Beach Tide Pools

Google Maps and SatNav/GPS Coordinates: 47.920627,-124.637643

The road to Rialto Beach leaves La Push Road at **Three Rivers Resort**, home of the **Treaty Line Sign** (Site #19). Turn northwest onto Mora Road, drive 5 miles to its end, park and head to the beach.

On the beach, turn right and walk north. Rialto's tide pool landmark is the distinctive **Hole-in-the-Wall** rock formation approximately 1.6 miles from the car parks. This formation separates Rialto into southern and northern beach coves.

Hole-in-the-Wall can only be accessed during low tide, but the beach in both coves remains safe to travel, even at high tide. If you find the beach sloggy to walk on, or you stumble in the rocky areas, scout for a driftwood pole to use as a walking stick.

[Internet-posted image segment (enhanced), ©2009 Michael Hanscom]

La Push First Beach—Site 21

About half-way to Rialto's tide pool area you'll reach the mouth of **Ellen Creek**. There are days during summer months when it doesn't extend to the ocean, and a thin strip of beach between creek and ocean can be traversed easily. At all other times of the year, the creek is bridged by gigantic driftwood logs. Use the widest ones to walk across. Alternatively, you can safely wade through the shallow mouth of Ellen Creek.

Please Note: This is the point where dogs can go no further north on Rialto Beach. Since dogs aren't allowed anywhere on Second Beach, you cannot go tidepooling with a canine Twi-companion.

When you reach Hole-in-the-Wall, start picking your way out to the farthest-from-shore areas found at the base of the **sea stack** beyond the hole.
http://en.wikipedia.org/wiki/Stack_%28geology%29

[Internet-posted image segment (enhanced), ©2011 ColorReversal]

At low tide, visitors can walk *through* Hole-in-the-Wall to Rialto's northern cove. Although tide pools are found in both coves, we strongly suggest popping to the northern cove only long enough to take a few pix there. If you linger on the north side of Hole-in-the-Wall for longer than a few minutes, stay alert for the returning tide!

[Internet-posted image segment (enhanced), ©2013 Aron Hess]

At the mid-point between low and high tide times, it becomes impossible to walk back through Hole-in-the-Wall and return to the southern cove's beach. Inattentive visitors have become trapped—for 6 hours or more—on the north side.

[Internet-posted image segment (enhanced), ©2012 Ricky Hazboy]

A strenuous overland trail exists between Rialto's north and south coves, but we do not know how well signed it is. It's best to simply avoid becoming trapped there by returning to the south side of the hole immediately after snapping a few pix.

[Internet-posted image (enhanced), ©December 2008 Bern Harrison]

Magnificent marine inhabitants are found in the tide pools on the south side of Hole-in-the-Wall. Twilighters who take time to go tidepooling at Rialto Beach will not be disappointed!

22

The Quileute Reservation and Old La Push Village

Where Jacob Grew Up
http://www.quileutenation.org/
https://www.facebook.com/pages/The-Quileute-Nation-of-LaPush-WA/197450675626
http://en.wikipedia.org/wiki/Quileute_people

Google Maps & SatNav/GPS: Provided below.

Hours of Operation: Vary

Visit Time: This depends entirely on how much you want to see and do.

- At minimum, schedule a **3.5 hour** visit. This allows for travel time between Forks and the Res, plus 15 minutes to snap exterior pix at each of the 8 primary Res locations.
- If you'd like to eat at the only Res restaurant, stop at the only Res gift shop, and step inside the only Res grocery store, schedule an additional 30 minutes (45 minutes) at each of these places—**5 hours**, total.
- Add another 30 minutes to snap exterior pix at the carving shed and Senior Center—**5.5 hours**.
- If you didn't do a TwiFoot tour, add yet another 30 minutes to snap exterior pix at the two Native art sites—**6 hours**.
- TTTS recommends **devoting an entire day** to your Quileute Reservation and old La Push village visit. That way, you'll have

plenty of time to *socialize* with friendly tribal members at the carving shed, the Senior Center, or anywhere else you encounter them. Trust us—you'll not be disappointed!

Res Locations within this Chapter:

1: Jacob's High School
  1a: Quileute Cultural Center for Carvers
2: The Old Quileute Tribal School,
  2a: Quileute Senior Center
3: Jacob's Childhood Community Center
4: River's Edge Restaurant
5: Quileute Harbor and Marina
6: Quileute Oceanside Resort Gift Shop
7: Lonesome Creek Grocery Store
  7a: Quileute Cemetery Gateway
8: Jacob's Teenage Community Center—the Akalat Center
  8a: Native Art Bus Shelter

Background

Prior to journeying anywhere on the Quileute Reservation, please read the **Indian Country Etiquette** page of the Quileute Nation's website.
http://www.quileutenation.org/indian-country-etiquette

It is important to be familiar with appropriate behavior specific to the Res, in addition to abiding by the **Twilighter Treaty**. For example, Quileute tribal law forbids picking up or removing any kind of object found on the Res. Such objects include—but are not limited to—sand, rocks, shells, minerals, marine growth, driftwood, eagle feathers, broken pottery, etc.

Please also peruse the **Quileute Media Policy**.
www.quileutenation.org/qtc/media_policy_2010.pdf

In that document, among other facts, you'll learn that:
- All artwork seen on the Res is copyrighted and should not be photographed without first obtaining the artist's permission.
- Camera or cell phone photography intended for personal use is generally allowed—*except* during dancing and singing performances.

Quilette Reservation & Old La Push Village—Site 22

- All audio and videotaping while on the Res is strictly prohibited, even if only intended for personal use.
- Capturing images or recording sounds during any form of Quileute performance—be it dancing, singing, or drumming—is strictly prohibited, unless prior authorization is obtained from the Quileute Tribal Council.

Twilighters interested in learning more about the Quileute Nation before visiting should explore *everything* available on the Quileute Nation website, particularly the history page.
http://www.quileutenation.org/history

Jacob's Village—Old La Push Village—is Moving!

The old La Push village is situated at the mouth of the Quileute River. It stretches east along the river's southern bank and south along the Pacific Ocean coastline (First Beach). The village was named by traders, based on Chinook Indian jargon meaning "river mouth"—a corruption of the French "la bouche."
http://en.wikipedia.org/wiki/La_Push,_Washington

The old village is subject to frequent river flooding, high coastal storm tides, and an ever-present tsunami danger. The safety of children attending the Quileute Tribal School, located only one foot above sea level, has been of particular concern. According to Rep. Norm Dicks, D-Port Angeles,

> "Although the tribe's reservation at La Push is spectacularly beautiful, it also is a dangerous place to live. The threat of tsunamis is a harsh reality that the Quileute Tribe faces every day."

In 2011, Dicks introduced a land-transfer bill in Congress, for the purpose of enabling relocation of tsunami-threatened tribal buildings to higher ground. After approval by the House and Senate, President Barack Obama signed the bill into law on February 27th, 2012, transferring 772 acres of Olympic National Park land to the Quileute Nation. Ironically, all of the transferred land was within territory originally owned by the Quileutes.

The gradual process of relocating Quileute tribal public services from buildings in the old village has already begun. Residents of 40 homes found in the tsunami-threatened area have been offered the opportunity to move to property on higher ground, but may remain where they are should they wish. The relocation project is not expected to be finished until 2017.
http://indiancountrytodaymedianetwork.com/article/quileute-is-moving-to-higher-ground-100321
http://www.dailykos.com/story/2013/02/28/1188893/-Tsunami-Geology-and-the-Quileute-Nation#

Tour the Twilight Saga Book One

What the Move Means to Twilighters

Unless destroyed by a Tsunami, we anticipate that all Jacob-related buildings in the old village will remain intact, even after the services provided within them have been moved to new buildings on higher ground. While planning your La Push visit, however, it would be wise to periodically visit the **Quileute Res Site #22 TwiLinks** PDF posted on our website. TwiLinks files are updated whenever we learn of new information.
http://TourTheTwilightSaga.com/B1/22TwiLinks.pdf

If you discover a Quileute Res update that we've missed—either during trip planning or site visiting—please report it on the **Tour the Twilight Saga Facebook** page so that your info can be shared with other Twilighters.
https://www.facebook.com/pages/Tour-The-Twilight-Saga/533851833326773

La Push Special Events

During **Stephenie Meyer Days** in September (info in our **Forks Prologue**), the Quileute Nation traditionally participates by hosting an event of some kind, such as the **Quileute Storytelling** session on First Beach in 2013. Twilighters unable to visit in September should go to the Quileute Nation's website and Facebook page to learn what special Res events may be scheduled during your holiday.

Annual events commonly held on the Quileute Res include:

- **Whale Welcoming Ceremony in mid-April.** This celebration honors the return of gray whales as they pass La Push during their spring migration from winter birthing grounds in Baja California, Mexico, to their summer habitat in Alaska's Bering Sea.
- **Quileute Days in mid-July.** Three days of Tribal Heritage events and displays, including a parade, dances and singing, games and tournaments, canoe racing, arts and crafts, and a traditional Quileute salmon bake.
- **Tribal Canoe Journey, July/August.** A tradition revived in 1989, over one hundred Northwest tribes and Canadian First Nations travel in canoes to bring their peoples together each year and celebrate their connection to salmon, the water, and each other. In recent years, members of international canoe cultures have joined the journey—some from as far away as New Zealand. Hosting of the annual event rotates among the Northwest and Canadian Native participants. Canoes leave from their homelands and travel to the host tribe's location. Depending on where the canoes start, the journey can last several weeks. A schedule is usually provided on the Quileute website, identifying the dates these amazingly beautiful traditional canoes can be seen sailing at La Push.

Quilette Reservation & Old La Push Village—Site 22

Quileute Tribal School History
http://www.quileutenation.org/government/tribal-school
http://www.quileute.bie.edu/community.htm
http://en.wikipedia.org/wiki/Quileute_Tribal_School

Traditionally, the Quileute people have excelled at educating their youth. In 1882, they were subjected to a U.S.-imposed tribal school system, introduced by a white man named A.W. Smith. His first act was to assign new names to every Quileute student based on characters from the Bible or American history as well as anglicizing Quileute place names. Thereafter, Smith adhered to U.S. doctrine by attempting to exterminate all aspects of the tribe's cultural heritage.

> "Boarding schools, forced religious conversion, and the reservation system aimed to 'kill the Indian, and save the man,' and made traditional practices and language difficult and even dangerous to practice. Children were beaten for speaking their Native languages in missionary schools."

http://www.burkemuseum.org/truth_vs_twilight/quileutes.php

Although these policies ceased sometime around 1920, the first tribal school intended to educate Quileute children in their cultural heritage wasn't established until 1971.

Today's Quileute tribal school system serves students from kindergarten through high school with its most important focus to **"protect, preserve, and enhance the Quileute language and culture for future generations."**

In 1977, for instance, only ten elderly tribal members were able to speak the Quileute language fluently. By 1992, that number had dwindled to three. Happily, the Quileute language has since become an integral part of the tribal school curriculum. Quileute children of all ages attend language lessons daily, and all tribal members are encouraged to use Quileute words and phrases as often as possible.

Quileute Reservation Sites

Places of Twilighter interest on the Res, and in the old La Push village, are listed in the order of most efficient travel following a visit to the north end of **First Beach** (Site #21). The first five sites we discuss are in the old village. These sites are within easy walking distance from **The Point** parking lot.

Tour the Twilight Saga Book One

[Bing map segments (married, enhanced), ©2013 Nokia/Microsoft Corp]

Tour the Twilight Saga's Old La Push Village Walking Tour Map is posted online within our Res Visit Maps
http://www.TourTheTwilightSaga.com/B1/22ResVisitMaps.pdf

Old La Push Village Walking Tour Map Key
    1: Jacob's High School
        1a: Quileute Tribal School Cultural Center for Carvers
    2: Old Quileute Tribal School
        2a: Quileute Senior Center
    3: Jacob's Childhood Community Center
    4: River's Edge Restaurant
    5: Quileute Harbor and Marina

[©2013 CD Miller]

Quilette Reservation & Old La Push Village—Site 22

Jacob's High School
Google Maps and SatNav/GPS: 47.908245,-124.638008

Two Quileute Tribal School buildings exist in La Push's old village. The more modern one opened in the early '80s and is located southeast of The Point car park, only a few feet above sea level. Like its predecessor, the school originally housed classrooms for all Quileute students, from kindergarten through the 12th grade of high school.

In 2001—long before 2012 land-transfer bill was signed—the Quileutes obtained grants that allowed them to begin construction of two new buildings safely situated far above the coastal Tsunami zone. A new community center was completed in 2002 (see the **Akalat Center** below) intended to house the high school classrooms. Soon after, a brand new primary school building was finished next door to the Akalat Center.

Bella moved back to Forks in January of 2005—the middle of her high school junior year. At that time, Jacob was a high school freshman. We cannot find records of when various grades' classrooms were moved from the old village's modern school building to the new facilities. It is probable, however, that Quileute high school students were still attending classes in the old village as late as 2011. Thus, we believe that Jacob attended high school in the old village's modern school building—*not* in the Akalat Center.

The Quileute Tribal School Cultural Center for Carvers

As chronicled in *Eclipse* chapter 17, Jacob gave Bella a high school graduation gift: a silver charm bracelet with a tiny, intricate wooden carving of a wolf attached.

> "I didn't make the bracelet," he admitted. "Just the charm." ...
> "It's something Billy taught me. He's better at it than I am."

Carving is essential to the Quileute culture. In 2009 the Tribal Council hired Master Carver David Wilson of the Lummi Tribe to teach the art of Northwest Native American wood carving to all Quileute students and tribal members interested in learning the skills.

> "Some of the various projects students and community members make include rattles, necklaces, paddles, and masks. Many of the students have persuaded their family members to accompany them to the carving shed after school or on the weekends. Carving has become a family activity for many."

http://www.quileutenation.org/newsletter/november_2011.pdf

Tour the Twilight Saga Book One

[©2013 Tara Miller]

The carving shed and canoe shelter are next to the modern school in old La Push village. If the carving center is closed when you visit, feel free to wander about, snapping personal pix of the colorful cedar canoes stored here, and discreetly peeking into the wood shop windows.

If students or community members are present, please observe the **Twilighter Treaty**.

Do not trespass on private property.
Do not disturb—or photograph—the residents.
Do not bite any humans, for any reason.

Walk up the school drive near the shed. Indicate your interest with a smile and a wave from the driveway, but do not actually approach unless someone invites you to. Even though you probably *will* be invited to join them, do not take photos of any people, and be sure to ask permission before snapping pix of the canoes or other artwork.

🚶 Going to Jacob's High School/Quileute Carving Center

Parking Lot SatNav/GPS Coordinates: 47.908245,-124.63981

Address Alternative (the **River's Edge Restaurant**):
  41 Main Street, La Push, WA 98305

Drive north of Forks on the main road, Hwy 101. Turn left at Hwy 110 and head west on La Push Road. Follow La Push Road as it winds west and north toward the coast, passing other Twilight Saga sites, until you reach the old La Push Village.

Yes, you'll pass several Twilight Saga sites on they way, and could visit them first. But, we believe it best to begin at the old village and then work your way back to Forks.

Quilette Reservation & Old La Push Village—Site 22

[©2013 Tara Miller]

La Push Road/Ocean Front Drive ends when it becomes Coast Guard Road—at the zebra-crossing seen above, flanked by a "NO THRU Traffic" sign. There, the main road leads you to the right, onto Alder Street.

Once on Alder Street, take the next left and drive north on River Street. At the end of River Street, turn left. Follow the road as it twists west until you see the Point C gravel parking lot with James Island perched beyond it. This old La Push Village area is called **The Point**. Head left and park in a spot closest to the car park's south side.

There is no fee for automobile parking at The Point.

According to our local guide, however, during special Quileute events you may be approached by a native individual asking you to pay her/him for parking. Should that happen, *just pay them*. They'll not ask for more than a buck or two, because they aren't sanctioned by the Quileute Council and won't want to generate complaints.

[Bing map segment (enhanced), ©2013 Nokia/Microsoft Corp]

If visiting the north end of First Beach prior to beginning your old village trek, exit the beach via the Signed Trail (the green dotted path seen above) when finished. Keep right after emerging at the modern school's drive and walk northeast to the carving shed and canoe shelter (**1a**).

189

Tour the Twilight Saga Book One

If not visiting the north end of First Beach, simply head southeast from The Point's car park and walk down the modern school's drive. Follow the drive when it curves left and you'll see the carving shed and canoe shelter ahead, to the right.

When finished at the carving shed, return to The Point car park. Snap photos of Jacob's High School (**1**) on the way.

[*Twilight in Forks* screenshot segment (enhanced)]

The Old Quileute Tribal School

Google Maps and SatNav/GPS: 47.908216,-124.636742

Only a 2 minute walk from The Point car park, the old Quileute Tribal School building is a small, two-story structure found at the northwest end of Coast Guard Road. This is where Quileute children of all grades attended school between 1971 and the early '80s. Although Jacob didn't attend classes here, history-loving Twilighters will find it interesting.

[Internet-posted photo (enhanced), ©2011 the Mittelstaedt Family]

The Quileute Senior Center

Hours of Operation: Monday-Thursday 10am to 5:30pm, 8am to 3pm on Fridays

http://www.quileutenation.org/seniors-program
http://www.quileutenation.org/seniors-program/senior-center

Quilette Reservation & Old La Push Village—Site 22

Less than a block southeast of the old tribal school is the Quileute Senior Center. Finished in 2004, this building is a marvelous example of modern Quileute architecture. If the center is open during your visit and you have time for more than exterior pic-snapping, pop in and strike up a conversation! According to the Senior Center's program manager, Lisa Hohman-Penn, most Quileute tribal elders thoroughly enjoy being visited by non-Natives— even if they're Twilighters. Not only are they happy to regale visitors with Quileute tribal stories, you may be treated to a tour of the center's small **Museum of Elder Artifacts.**

[Bing map segment (enhanced), ©2013 Nokia/Microsoft Corp]

🚶 Going to the Old Tribal School and Quileute Senior Center

> **Please Note:** It is possible to reach the old tribal school building by walking *through* the modern school's campus. It is best, however, not to violate that space.

From The Point's car park, head northeast along Main Street, following the road as it curves right. Turn right at the driveway leading down from Coast Guard Road—the "do not enter" sign applies only to automobile traffic. Walk up the drive until you reach the front of the old Tribal School building (**2**) and snap your pix.

Please observe the **Twilighter Treaty** and do not enter the old school building.

To snap exterior Quileute Senior Center pix (**2a**)—or venture inside and visit with tribal elders—continue a little farther southeast on Coast Guard Road (the green dotted path seen above) and turn left into the Senior Center's car park.

When finished in this area, retrace your steps back down the Coast Guard Road exit drive. Turn left to return to your car. Turn right to walk to the other La Push village sites.

Tour the Twilight Saga Book One

[©2013 Tara Miller]

The Old Quileute Community Center

Google Maps and SatNav/GPS: 47.909309,-124.637254
30 River St, La Push WA 98350

Prior to completion of the Akalat Center in 2002, all tribal events and activities were held in the old Quileute Community Center. Thus, this building is where Jacob attended events such as drum circles and tribal dances when he was a child.

As seen in the photo above, the old community center has suffered significant storm damage, especially within the last decade. The wooden beams stretching across the building's second floor windows were installed to anchor the roof after it was detached and almost swept away by high winds in 2012.

The old Quileute Community Center is still used, but only during special events held in the old village. During the 2013 Paddle to Quinault canoe journey, for instance, vendor booths selling Native art, crafts, clothing, and food were there.
http://www.peninsuladailynews.com/article/20130728/NEWS/307289992/quileute-plan-two-day-celebration-before-final-stretch-for-canoe

Twihards divinely inspired to go *inside* Jacob's childhood community center will need to schedule a visit during an old La Push village Quileute event.

[©2013 Tara Miller] [©2013 CD Miller]

Quilette Reservation & Old La Push Village—Site 22

River's Edge Restaurant
http://forkswa.com/listing/rivers-edge-restaurant/

Google Maps and SatNav/GPS: 41 Main Street, La Push, WA 98350
47.909309,-124.637254

Hours of Operation: 8am to 9pm, 7 days a week during the summer season; may be closed during winter months.

River's Edge is the only restaurant on the Res. It occupies a renovated building that once was the original Quileute River Coast Guard Station boathouse (1929), and lies across the street from the old Quileute Community Center.

If seated at the restaurant's northeastern windows—the tables on your right as you enter—you'll look out over the Quileute Marina while dining. If you walk straight ahead after entering, following the floor as it slants down toward the opposite wall, you may be seated at a northwestern window table. From there you'll enjoy a magical view of the Quileute River mouth. Remnants of the old boat landing ramp (seen in the pic above right) still stretch to the water from the building's northwest wall. In fact, the boat landing ramp is the reason the restaurant's floor slants downward.

Happily, remarkable marine inhabitants can be viewed from any River's Edge Restaurant window table. Bald eagles are often sighted in May, golden eagles in June. Brown pelicans, river otters, or sea lions may be seen during almost every month of the year.

As for the food and service: based on TripAdvisor reviews, it seems to be a crapshoot. In September of 2013, Chas and Tara of TTTS were far too absorbed by the view from our table's window to pay much attention to the quality of food or service. If either had been horrendous, however, we surely would have noticed. Bottom Line: Chas and Tara were perfectly happy with the food and service at River's Edge Restaurant.

[©2013 Tara Miller]

Tour the Twilight Saga Book One

The Quileute Harbor Marina
http://www.quileutenation.org/business/marina

Google Maps and SatNav/GPS: 71 Main St, La Push, WA 98350

If you walk a block northeast of River's Edge Restaurant you'll arrive at the Quileute harbor and marina. Home to commercial fishing boats as well as recreational vessels, a business of particular interest to Twilighters is found here: **Pacific Coast Charter.**

> "**Twilight Tour.** Come aboard the *Ali Lynn* and experience the Twilight hot spots of La Push from the water. The tour includes a view of La Push, 1st & 2nd beach and wraps up with a stunning view of Jacob and Bella's cliff (the cliff Bella jumps off of in [the novel] New Moon). The cliff is only visible from the water and is located at the end of second beach."

They also offer whale watching excursions and private fishing tours.
http://pacificcoastcharter.org/

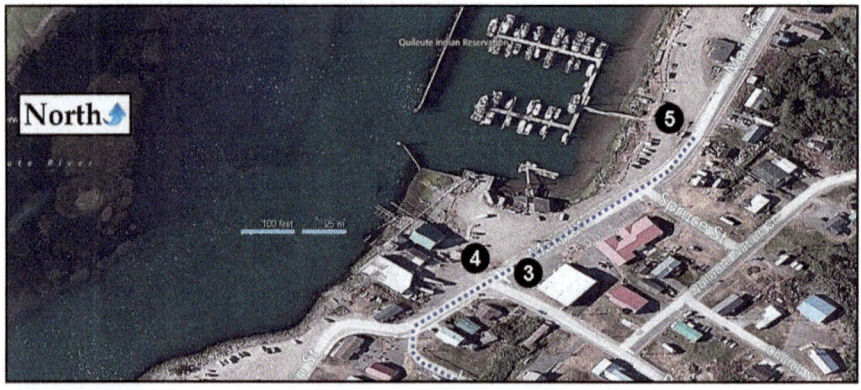

[Bing map segment (enhanced), ©2013 Nokia/Microsoft Corp]

🚶 Going to Jacob's Childhood Community Center, River's Edge Restaurant, and La Push Marina

Head northeast on Main Street from The Point's car park or the Coast Guard Road exit drive. At the first intersection (River Street) you'll see the old Quileute Community Center on your right, and River's Edge Restaurant on your left.

After enjoying these two sites, resume walking northeast on Main Street to reach the Marina. When finished in old La Push village, return to the car park.

Quilette Reservation & Old La Push Village—Site 22

Leave old La Push village by driving back the way you came.

The remaining Res sites of Twilighter interest lie between old La Push village and Forks. We provide written driving directions for reaching them below, and have created a map indicating their locations. Our Res Locations map is posted online within the same PDF that contains our Old La Push Village Walking Tour Map.

[Bing map segment (enhanced), ©2013 Nokia/Microsoft Corp]

Tour the Twilight Saga's Res Locations Map
http://www.TourTheTwilightSaga.com/B1/22ResVisitMaps.pdf

Res Locations Map Key

    1—5: These sites are identified on the **Old La Push Village Walking Tour Map**.
    6: Quileute Oceanside Resort Gift Shop
    7: Lonesome Creek Grocery Store
        7a: Quileute Cemetery Gateway
    8: Jacob's Teenage Community Center—the Akalat Center
        8a: Native Art Bus Shelter

The Quileute Oceanside Resort
http://www.quileuteoceanside.com/
https://www.facebook.com/QuileuteOceansideResort
http://forkswa.com/listing/quileute-oceanside-resort/

Google Maps and SatNav/GPS: 47.906332,-124.632257
    330 Ocean Drive, La Push, WA 98350

★This address is problematic for Google Maps and TomToms. Use the coordinates.

Gift Shop Hours: 8am to 10 pm during the summer season; 8am to 8 pm in winter.

[©2013 CD Miller]

The Quileute Oceanside Resort is owned and operated by the Quileute Nation and is the only place that offers lodging options *on* the Res. You'll reach the main office building (above) about 2 minutes after beginning your drive back to Forks.

[©2013 Tara Miller]

Non-lodgers are welcome at the Oceanside Resort Gift Shop, which is located in the main office building. This shop offers a small collection of Native art work, such as wood carvings and jewelry, as well as clothing and souvenirs sporting Native designs. The resort's **Native Grounds Espresso** hut (below, right) is next to the main office.

Quilette Reservation & Old La Push Village—Site 22

[©2013 CD Miller]

Twilighters who lodge at the Quileute Oceanside Resort will find First Beach right outside the door of every accommodation. One, two, and three bedroom beach-side cabins are available—including the **Wolf Den**, a two bedroom cabin dedicated to Jacob Black.
http://www.quileuteoceanside.com/accommodations-overview

[©2013 CD Miller]

Two large motel buildings—The Thunderbird and The Whale—offer luxury or standard accommodation options. Luxury rooms have a beach view and full kitchens. Standard rooms have kitchenettes and a parking lot view.

> **Please Note:** Televisions and telephones are *not* available in any of the Oceanside's motel rooms or cabins, "in order to better facilitate your escape from the chaos of the outside world." Happily, a WiFi access room is located within the resort's main office building.

The Oceanside Resort also has 5 tent campsites and 42 full hook-up RV spaces situated on the beach, each with its own picnic table and fire pit.

Tour the Twilight Saga Book One

[©2013 Tara Miller]

Lonesome Creek Store
http://www.quileutenation.org/business/lonesome-creek

Google Maps & SatNav/GPS: 47.904289,-124.629661
490 Ocean Dr, La Push, WA 98350 (Another problematic address for TomTom.)

Hours of Operation: 6am to 10pm in summer; 7am to 9pm in winter.

The only grocery store on the Res, Lonesome Creek is less than a 1 minute drive (5 minute walk) south of the Oceanside Resort office. Quileute owned and operated, it also has a few gifts and souvenirs. If you didn't bring your own firewood, buy it here. Public restrooms are also available here.

[©2013 Tara Miller]

Quilette Reservation & Old La Push Village—Site 22

Quileute Cemetery Gateway

https://www.facebook.com/media/set/?set=a.10152918860135627.1073741830.197450675626&type=3

Google Maps & SatNav/GPS: 47.902505,-124.62773

Two-tenths of a mile southeast of Lonesome Creek store is the beautifully carved and painted Quileute Cemetery gateway. Completed in June of 2013 by Israel Shotridge, a talented Tlingit Native artist, its two 15-foot totem poles support a 30-foot long canoe façade. Shotridge reports that the images he carved were inspired by drawings done by Quileute schoolchildren in the early 1900s—drawings displayed in the Seattle Art Museum's Quileute Exhibit between August 2010 and August 2011.

Twilight tour busses are authorized to stop here, but there is no space available for public parking at the gateway. If you didn't enjoy this photo op while on a tour, it's only a 3 minute walk from Lonesome Creek store.

Please abide by the **Twilighter Treaty** and Quileute Nation Etiquette when visiting the entrance to this sacred site. **Do not pass *through* the gateway.** Only tribal members and those they personally invite are allowed within. Do not photograph or disturb any individuals who may be present during your visit.

Approximately one minute after leaving Lonesome Creek store and resuming the drive back toward Forks you'll pass the parking lots for **Second Beach** (info in Site #21). In another minute, you'll reach the intersection of By-Yak-Way and La Push Road.

[©2013 Tara Miller]

Turn right on By-Yak-Way and you'll see the **Akalat Center** sign next to the La Push Police Department. Drive past the sign and turn right onto By-Yak Loop to reach the modern Quileute Community Center.

Tour the Twilight Saga Book One

[©2013 Tara Miller]

The Akalat Center
http://www.quileute.bie.edu/akalat.htm

Google Maps and SatNav/GPS: The Center's address is unpublished. Coordinates for the Center; 47.89724,-124.617194

Hours of Operation: Undetermined

After a year of construction, and at a cost of $3.7 million, the Akalat Center was completed in 2002. As you can see, it is gorgeous!

> "The building's architecture reflects unique aspects of Quileute heritage, values and identity with the goal of promoting tribal healing and pride. A series of shed roofs at different elevations is meant to evoke the traditional Quileute ceremonial longhouse design and the action of the ocean, central to Quileute life. Large beams projecting from the upper roofline recall seagoing canoes cresting a wave."

http://www.apawood.org/level_b.cfm?content=app_com_school

Since the Akalat Center's opening, the majority of La Push community activities have been held here, within its large, state-of-the-art Tribal School gymnasium. This is where Jacob attended gatherings when he was a teen.

The Akalat Center also houses some school classrooms, a commercially-equipped kitchen, high-tech meeting facilities, and tribal cultural displays.

If you have the good fortune to be visiting the Res on a Wednesday, non-Native visitors are welcome to attend the weekly Quileute **potluck dinner** (bring something!) and **Healing Circle/Drum Group** session from 5 to 9:30pm.

> **Please Note:** As of November, 2013, the Quileute Nation website continues to describe these Wednesday night gatherings as taking

Quilette Reservation & Old La Push Village—Site 22

place at the old La Push village Quileute Community Center. Forks residents, however, insist that they have been held in the Akalat Center's gym since 2002.

When heading to attend a potluck drum circle, stop at the Akalat Center first. If it isn't being held here, you can continue to the old village's community center without delay.

After enjoying the Akalat Center, return to By-Yak-Way, turn left and head back toward La Push Road. There, turn right and drive into the **bus stop area** on the intersection's southwest corner.

[©2013 Tara Miller]

Native Art Bus Shelter
http://www.youtube.com/watch?v=Lz4HM8Gmq74

Google Maps and SatNav/GPS: 47.897255,-124.614855

In 2011, master carver CHiXapkaid (Michael Pavel) and his "House of Swasulayas" team of carvers were commissioned to create a bus shelter for the Quileute people.

Equipped with lights and a heating system, the Quileute refer to the shelter as a **Warm House**. It is constructed entirely from cedar—including the bench—and designed in the manner of a traditional (albeit shorter) Quileute **Long House**.

The magnificently carved totems (stylized images) that adorn it represent spirit animals special to the Quileutes. At the bottom of the shelter's two square front posts is an Earth Spirit animal totem: the raccoon. At the top of the posts, and on the back wall, are Air Spirit animal totems: the raven and the eagle. Beneath the eagle on the back wall is the whale, a Water Spirit animal totem. Exquisitely etched into glass panels on either end is the Wolf

Tour the Twilight Saga Book One

Spirit totem—symbolizing instinct, intelligence, an appetite for freedom, and an awareness of the importance of social connections.
http://en.wikipedia.org/wiki/Totem
http://www.spiritanimal.info/wolf-spirit-animal/

TwiFoot tours schedule an educational photo-op stop at the bus shelter. According to Rosemary:

> "Historically, the Quileute people carved and painted spirit totems, but did not create totem *poles*. Totem poles didn't exist on the Res until after tourists began clamoring for them. The Warm House's Quileute totems are far more culturally-accurate than the totem poles seen elsewhere."

When finished at the Warm House, resume driving east on La Push Road to reach Forks or your next Twilight Saga Tour destination.

23

The Westlands Homestead

The *Original* Cullen House
http://www.thecabinsatbeavercreek.com/
http://forkswa.com/listing/the-cabins-at-beaver-creek/

Address: 272 Rixon Road, Sappho, WA 98305

Google Maps & SatNav/GPS Coordinates: 48.071498,-124.288291

Hours of Operation: This is a private residence. Please do not approach the house unless you're there to check into a booked Beaver Creek Cabin.

Visit Time: Schedule 20 minutes to snap exterior pix as a non-lodger.

Westlands Homestead is the home of **John and Michelle Simpson**, who own and operate four vacation rental cabins on their property: **The Cabins at Beaver Creek**. More importantly—to Twilighters—Westlands Homestead is the real-world structure that inspired Stephenie Meyer's descriptions of the **Cullen House**.

Stephenie selected Forks as the setting for her first novel sight-unseen, but managed to visit the town more than a year before *Twilight* was published.

> "In the summer of 2004 I snuck up to Forks to check it out; it was the first time I've ever been to any part of Washington. I took my sister Emily with me—she was a really great sport considering that she was seven months pregnant at the time."

http://stepheniemeyer.com/twilight_forks.html

Tour the Twilight Saga Book One

According to the *Twilight Territory* guidebook (©2009, Forks Forum Newspaper / Olympic View Publishing LLC):

> "When Meyer visited Forks in 2004 during the writing of *Twilight*, a large 'historic home for sale' sign directed interested buyers and the curious to the home, which is known on the West End as Westlands. At the same time, detailed photographs of Westlands were posted on the Web site of Forks real estate firm Lunsford & Associates. There is speculation that the author either drove up to the house or possibly viewed it on the Lunsford & Associates Web site and used it as a model for the Cullen family home. Like the Cullen house, Westlands is located well outside of Forks, along a river in a secluded spot. The centerpiece of the Westlands estate is a stately home built in the early 1900s..."

Real-world Westlands Homestead attributes reflected in Stephenie's Cullen House descriptions are found in the following *Twilight* novel quotes.

> "I realized, as he drove my truck out of the main part of town, that I had no idea where he lived. We passed over the bridge at the Calawah River, the road winding northward, ... then we were past the other houses altogether, driving through misty forest. I was trying to decide whether to ask or be patient, when he turned abruptly onto an unpaved road. It was unmarked, barely visible among the ferns."

The Calawah River lies between the central area of Forks and La Push Road (Hwy 110). To reach anyplace north of Forks, you must drive north on Hwy 101 and cross the **Calawah River bridge**.

Between La Push Road and Sappho—the next town north of Forks on Hwy 101—there are only a handful of houses.

To reach Westlands Homestead from Forks, you must drive approximately 11 miles north of La Push Road on Hwy 101, then turn abruptly left onto a barely visible, single-lane road, immediately after crossing the third **Sol Duc River** bridge.

The Westlands Homestead—Site 23

Westlands Homestead
[©2013 Tara Miller]

The Westlands Homestead house looks almost exactly the same as Stephenie's physical description of the Cullen House.

> "The trees held their protecting shadow right up to the walls of the house that rose among them, making obsolete the deep porch that wrapped around the first story. The house was timeless, graceful, and probably a hundred years old. It was painted a soft, faded white, three stories tall, rectangular and well proportioned. The windows and doors were either part of the original structure or a perfect restoration. ...
>
> "I could hear the river close by, hidden in the obscurity of the forest. ... [Edward's window] looked down on the winding Sol Duc River, across the untouched forest to the Olympic Mountain range."

Originally constructed over 100 years ago as the Olympic Peninsula headquarters for Clallam Lumber Company, the Westlands Homestead house is situated in a forest clearing only 500 feet from the Sol Duc River. The sound of water rushing over river rocks can be heard everywhere on the property.

> **Please Note:** The Cullen House exterior scenes you might be familiar with from the films were shot on location in **Portland, Oregon** (TTTS Book Three). While this home is incredibly beautiful, it looks nothing like the novel's Cullen House description.

Tour the Twilight Saga Book One

[*Twilight* screenshot (enhanced)]

Additional Westlands Homestead History

Called "the Pathfinder in the Wilderness" by area historians, Theodore (Teddy) Rixon spent many years exploring and surveying the Olympic Peninsula with his partner, Arthur Dodwell. The U.S. Department of the Interior published their first collection of scientific field notes in 1900; *The Olympic Forest Reserve, Washington*.

Because he also was a talented and well-educated engineer, the Clallam Lumber Company hired Teddy to administrate their Olympic Peninsula logging operations. When it was finished, Teddy and his family moved into the company's new headquarters building, Westlands Homestead.

Westlands Homestead, approximately 1916
[Forks Timber Museum Digital Collection photo segment (enhanced)]

Sometime around 1920, the company moved its headquarters elsewhere. Teddy decided to stay on and purchased the Westlands Homestead property from them.

The Westlands Homestead—Site 23

Many locals still refer to the home as the **Rixon House**, especially because it resides on **Rixon Road**. Although the road *was* named after Teddy, the Rixons always referred to their home as the "Westlands Homestead."

Teddy and his wife, Caroline, had an adopted daughter named Gertrude, but everyone called her Bunny. In 1926, Bunny married Teddy's nephew, Robert Rixon, in a ceremony held at Westlands Homestead. After the wedding, the elder Rixons relocated to Port Angeles and the newlywed Rixons moved into the Westlands house.

It was Bunny's idea to build cabins on the property and rent them to visiting hunters and fishermen. Small and simply-constructed, Bunny managed the nine original Westlands Homestead cabins until the fall of 1948, when she and Robert moved to Salt Spring Island, north of Victoria, British Columbia.

Fast forward to 2005 when Michele and John Simpson were in the market for a house. The Simpsons never saw the real estate notice found by Stephenie Meyer the year before. Instead, they were driving around Clallam County and looking at other properties when Michele suddenly spied a dilapidated, old sign, teetering in the weeds beside Rixon Road's obscure Hwy 101 entrance. It read, "Historic House for Sale." She immediately directed John to drive down the lane.

> "When we reached the house I got out of the car, did a 360, and fell in love."

After purchasing the Westlands Homestead property, John and Michelle honored its history by retaining the name preferred by the Rixons.

On Saturday, March 21st, 2009—the very day that the *Twilight* DVD was released—the Westlands Homestead house was gutted by a horrible fire.

[*Twilight in Forks* screenshot segments (enhanced) above and below]

John and Michelle were devastated by the loss of their home. But, rather than using the insurance settlement to build a modern house in its place, the Simpsons elected to pursue a far more expensive and time-consuming option. They decided to rebuild Westlands Homestead as close to its original design and material content as possible.

From an article in the Spring 2011 edition of *Living on the Peninsula* magazine:

> "John, knowledgeable about fine woodworking and quality lumber selection, chose Port Angeles-based woodworkers Ben Simmons and Curtis Hansen for the framing and finish carpentry. ... To utilize local products for rebuilding the house, the fine, straight, vertical-grained fir for the interior woodwork came from the mill of McLanahan Lumber south of Forks. Sequim cabinet maker Jesse Bay crafted the Douglas-fir cabinets and milled the beautiful interior woodwork. Mason Pete Bliven of Blitz Masonry in Sequim replicated Westland's original river-rock fireplace and chimney by copying details found in old photos of the home."
> http://issuu.com/leader/docs/lopspring2011

The project took approximately two years to complete. Modern safety features (such as fire stops), as well as 21st-century kitchen appliances and bathroom fixtures were installed. All other restoration work, however, was accomplished in a manner that faithfully retained the home's original appearance. Thus, the Westlands Homestead house looks exactly the same as it did when Stephenie penned her Cullen House description in 2004.

The Westlands Homestead—Site 23

[©2013 Tara Miller]

Westlands Homestead is a Private Residence

John and Michelle are well aware of their home's important Twilight Saga association, however, they don't actively promote it. Happily, they're extremely friendly people who are not at all bothered by non-lodging Twilighters driving up Rixon Road to take pix of the Cullen House—as long as you don't go near the house and rental cabins, or traipse around their property uninvited.

If coming here as a non-lodger, please abide by the **Twilighter Treaty**, so that other non-lodging Twilighters can continue to enjoy this site long after you've gone.

Drive down Rixon Road until you near its end and see the Cullen House on the right. Pull into the *mouth* of the circular drive in front of it, but do not actually drive up to the house. Stay beside your car when taking photos. When finished, back out onto the road and return to Hwy 101.

The Cabins at Beaver Creek

Sadly, all of the original Bunny Rixon cabins disintegrated and disappeared long before the Simpsons arrived. But, John and Michelle recognized Westlands Homestead as being a perfect base for visiting the western area of the Olympic Peninsula, just as Bunny did. Only a 12 minute drive from Forks, a 30 minute drive from La Push or Rialto Beach, Westlands Homestead also is the perfect base for touring Twilighters.

In 2010 the Simpsons built four brand spanking new rental cabins. Far more substantial than Bunny's huts, two are single-storey structures that sleep up to four persons, two have a second floor loft and can accommodate up to six people.

Worried that visitors would have difficulty with the river's name, John and Michelle named their cabins after **Beaver Creek**—a Sol Duc River tributary unique to the property, that winds along its western border.

[©2013 Tara Miller]

Because all four cabins face the river, only their rather plain-looking backsides can be seen from Rixon Road.

[©2013 Tara Miller]

From the front, however, the Beaver Creek Cabins are absolutely gorgeous. Each has a covered porch and an elegant, incredibly comfortable, fully-equipped interior. Cabin 4 (above) has a ramp for wheelchair accessibility.

Chas and Tara so thoroughly enjoyed our stay here in 2013, that the very first **Tour the Twilight Saga YouTube video** Chas created was of Westlands Homestead and the Cabins at Beaver Creek.

The Westlands Homestead—Site 23

[©2013 Tara Miller]

In the TTTS vid, you'll see several shots of the property, the cabins, and the people-friendly animals that live here. Walk-through film footage of our cabin's interior is followed by a real-time trek to the Sol Duc River—less than 2 minutes from the porch.
http://www.youtube.com/watch?v=6Ja4cNp5yL8

[©2013 Tara Miller, above and below]

When not meditating on the riverbank or communing with members of the Simpson's menagerie, lodgers can also enjoy a scenic walk along the gentle paths that wind through the property's rainforest.

Tour the Twilight Saga Book One

[©2013 Tara Miller]

Oh, yeah. As if a convenient area location, 5-star accommodations, rainforest and riverside rambles weren't enough of an enticement to stay here, John and Michelle host a grand campfire gathering each night. Meet your fellow lodgers and share stories while snacking on John's gourmet S'mores. (Seriously ... he has a very special technique!)

By now, it should come as no surprise that Tour the Twilight Saga *highly* recommends lodging at Beaver Creek Cabins.

Here's what we suggest:

- Stay at the **Miller Tree Inn** (Site #10) — aka the Cullen House in Forks — on one night of your Twilight Saga Forks and La Push holiday, so that you can enjoy the Bragers' many Twilight-related amenities and a scrumptious breakfast.
- On all other nights of your visit, stay in a Beaver Creek Cabin. If your party consists of three to six persons, lodging here is quite economical. Best of all, if you book a Beaver Creek Cabin you'll be able to wander everywhere on the real-world Cullen House property at your leisure.

The Westlands Homestead—Site 23

[©2013 Tara Miller]

🛏 Lodging at Beaver Creek Cabins

In case you require more than our endorsement, **TripAdvisor** and **Yelp** reviews posted by others who have lodged here over the years are overwhelmingly positive.
http://www.tripadvisor.com/ShowUserReviews-g58476-d1862515-r170373085-The_Cabins_at_Beaver_Creek-Forks_Washington.html
http://www.yelp.com/biz/the-cabins-at-beaver-creek-beaver-3

> **Please Note:** When you arrive to check in, park up by the porch and go to the little Office attached to the west (left) side of the house.

🚗 Going To Westlands Homestead:

Google Maps SatNav/GPS Address: 272 Rixon Road, Sappho, WA 98305

Coordinates for the Hwy 101/Rixon Road turn: 48.069706,-124.283109

When driving to Westlands Homestead from points north, such as Port Angeles, you'll have no difficulty using either the address or coordinates above to find it.

When driving here from Forks or other points south, however, Google Maps doesn't think you can turn left immediately after crossing the 3rd Sol Duc River bridge. If your SatNav/GPS device is similarly confused, it may send you *several miles* past Rixon Road before directing you to turn around.

If heading to Westlands Homestead from Forks or La Push, follow our driving directions (below) and the Westlands Homestead Maps we posted on the TTTS website.

Tour the Twilight Saga Book One

Tour the Twilight Saga Westlands Homestead Maps
[Google Maps segments, married & enhanced, ©2013 Google
Bing map segment (enhanced), ©2013 Nokia/Microsoft Corp]
http://www.TourTheTwilightSaga.com/B1/23WestlandsMaps.pdf

TTTS Westlands Homestead Maps Key:
A: Forks Chamber of Commerce
B: La Push Road (Hwy 110) intersection with Hwy 101
C: Rixon Road intersection with Hwy 101
D: Westlands Homestead house at the end of Rixon Road

Directions to Westlands Homestead from Forks

Drive north from Forks on the main road, Hwy 101. After passing the La Push Road (Hwy 110) intersection, count the number of times you cross the **Sol Duc River**. After crossing the *second* Sol Duc River bridge, slow down. The left turn onto Rixon Road is immediately after the *third* Sol Duc River bridge—only half a mile beyond the second bridge.

[©2013 Tara Miller]

The Westlands Homestead—Site 23

If you become distracted by the gorgeous scenery and lose count of the Sol Duc bridges crossed, not to worry. About 10 minutes beyond La Push Road, watch for the "Entering Sappho" sign. Cross the next bridge and turn left at its end.

[©2013 Tara Miller]

If you miss the Rixon Road turn when driving north, take the next left onto Burnt Mountain Road and turn around. When south-bound on Hwy 101, Rixon Road is the little lane on the right, just before the Sol Duc bridge south of Burnt Mountain Road.

The End

Thus ends the adventures of tour the twilight saga book one. Please join us in vancouver, british columbia for book two.

Index

A

Akalat Center 59, 200
Andros
  Lissy viii
A Novel Holiday iv
Argosy Cruises Harbor Tour 11

B

Bella Burger 132
Bella Italia Restaurant 42
Bella's Tide Pools 161
Biers
  Riley 13, 14
Bingham
  Marcia viii, 63, 76
Bromann
  Val 24
Burke
  Billy 107

C

Cabins at Beaver Creek 209
Carson
  D. C. vii, viii
Colandrea
  Jennifer viii
  Nino viii, 120
  Rosemary viii, 44, 104, 120
Cross-Leppell
  Charlene 100
Cullen Graduation Cap Collage 111
Cullen House 56, 109

D

Dale
  Ben vii
  Karen Stoehr vii
Damascus Carver Café 90
Dazzled by Twilight 121
Dazzled By Twilight 67
Dazzled by Twilight Store 48
Décor d' Forks 145
Destee-Nation 21, 22

E

Edward's Practice Piano 111
Elwha River Casino 77
EMP Museum 11

F

First Beach 161
Forever in Forks 66
Forks Chamber of Commerce viii, 55, 56, 59, 72, 75
Forks Coffee Shop 56, 89
Forks Community Hospital 56, 133
Forks High School 93
Forks High School Sign 56
Forks High School Spartans Sign 95
Forks Outfitters 85
Forks Outfitters & the Thriftway 56
Forks Police Department 56, 105
Fork's Thriftway 85
Forks Timber Museum 72, 80
Fork's TwiFoot Tours viii
Forks Welcome Sign 60
Fremont Neighborhood 24
Fremont Sunday Street Market 26

Tour the Twilight Saga Book One

G

Google Maps iv
Gottschalks Department Store 51

H

Hachette Book Group iii
Hardwicke
   Catherine 1
Healing Circle 60
Hoh Rainforest 120
Hoh Rain Forrest 81
hriftway Espresso Bar 92
Hughes
   Janet 129
   Tom 129
Hutchison
   Carol viii
   Matt viii

J

Jacob & Bella's Beach 161
Jacob Black's House 59, 155, 156
Jacob's High School 187
Jenks
   J. 9, 20
JT's Baked Stuffs 127
JT's Sweet Stuffs 56, 127

L

La Push First Beach 59, 161
La Push Second Beach 59
Leppell's Flowers and Gifts 99
Leppell's Flowers & Gifts 56
Lincoln Theatre 47
Little, Brown and Company iii
Lonesome Creek Store 59, 198

M

McDonalds 51
Meyer
   Stephanie iii, 13, 42, 76

Michael's Seafood and Steakhouse 45
Miller
   Charly D. iv
   Tara vii, viii
Miller Tree Inn 56, 109
Mocha Motion Espresso 91
Museum of Flight 11

N

Native Art Bus Shelter 201
Native to Twilight 56
Native to Twilight Store 115
Newton's Olympic Outfitters 85
Northwest Folklife Festival 11
Number 4 Privet Drive 9

O

Oceanside Resort Gift Shop 59
Old La Push Village 181, 183
Old Mill Trading Post 59, 143
Old Quileute Community Center 192
Old Quileute Tribal School 190
Old Village 59
Olympic Peninsula 2
Original Cullen House 203

P

Pacific Science Center 11
Pike Place Market 9, 14
Pike Pub & Brewery 18
Port Book and News 50

Q

Quileute Cemetery Gateway 199
Quileute Days 184
Quileute Harbor Marina 194
Quileute Nation Treaty Line 149
Quileute Oceanside Resort 195
Quileute Reservation 181
Quileute Senior Center 190

Index

Quileute Tribal School 185
Quileute Tribal School Cultural
    Center for Carvers 187

R

Rialto Beach 59, 165
Rialto Beach Tide Pools 176
River's Edge Restaurant 193
Round House 143, 146
Russell Road 141

S

Seafair Summer Festival 11
Seattle Aquarium 11
Seattle International Film Festival 11
Seattle PrideFest 11
Simpson
  John viii, 203
  Michelle viii, 203
Site Rating Icons 3
Soroptimist International Garden 81
Space Needle 11
Spomer
  Ron viii
Squatchers 120
Stand Up 2 Cancer 67
Stephenie Meyer Day Celebration 63
Stephenie Meyer Days 184
Sully's Drive-In 56, 131
Summit Entertainment iv
Summit Entertainment, iii
Swan House 56, 137

T

Team Forks Twilight Tour 99
Team Forks Twilight Tours 101
Three Rivers Resort 149
Thriftway Espresso Café 87
Time Warner Book Group iii
Travel Tips 4

Treaty Line Sign 59
Tribal Canoe Journey 184
TwiFoot Store 125
TwiFoot Tours 56, 119
Twilight Bus Tours 61
Twilighter Treaty 2
Twilight Saga iii
Twilight Tide Pools 174
Twilight Tours 119
Twilight T-Shirt Trek 9, 21

U

uileute Reservation 59

V

Victoria's Newborn Army 9

W

Washington
  Aberdeen 2
  Forks 55, 71, 75, 89, 93, 99, 105, 109, 115, 127, 131, 133, 137, 141, 143, 149
  La Push 55, 161
  Port Angeles 41
  Sappho 203
  Seattle 2, 9
Westlands Homestead viii, 203
Whale Welcoming Ceremony 184
Wikimedia vii
Wikipedia vii
wilight Punch 132
Wolf Den 59, 155, 159
Woodland Park Zoo 11

Tour the Twilight Saga Book One

www.ingramcontent.com/pod-product-compliance
Lightning Source LLC
Chambersburg PA
CBHW070533170426
43200CB00011B/2412